Control and Security
of E-Commerce

Control and Security of E-Commerce

Gordon E. Smith

WILEY

John Wiley & Sons, Inc.

Library of Congress Cataloging-in-Publication Data:

Smith, Gordon E. (Gordon Edward)
    Control and security of e-commerce / Gordon E. Smith.
        p.   cm.
    Includes index.
    ISBN 0-471-18090-4 (CLOTH)
    1. Electronic commerce—Security measures. 2. Business
enterprises—Computer networks—Security measures. I. Title.
    HF5548.32.S5943   2004
    658.8'4—dc21   2003014145

Contents

Preface

This book is intended to provide a step by step approach to auditing and securing the E-commerce environment. As this is a very large topic, I have specifically broken it down into modules that will enable you to use a structured and proven approach. If you perform your E-commerce review in the same sequence as this book, you will cover all of the major control areas, using a peeling-the-onion approach. You will be able to focus on what needs to be done and concentrate on completing your review in a timely manner.

I am a strong believer in risk-based reviews. I also believe that a great deal of time can be saved if a series of checklists are used to provide background to the security analyst or auditor prior to beginning the actual project field work. For this reason, many of the chapters contain risk/control tables and checklists at the end of each section. The risk/control tables will assist you in understanding what can go wrong and provide a sample control to mitigate the risk. These are the same risk/control tables that we use as a starting point for all of Canaudit's E-commerce audits. Most of our clients are able to use them unaltered. As a side benefit, they can also be converted into a report format. Simply change the column headings from "Risks" to "Business Issues" and from "Controls" to "Suggested Actions" and you have much of your report prewritten. It will still have to be tailored to your environment; however you are much further ahead than starting from scratch.

The checklists may also need to be modified. Using the Canaudit approach, we send the checklists to the clients about 40 days before the start of the field work. They should be able to turn them around and get them back to you in about two weeks. You can then review the completed checklists and modify your approach based on the knowledge you glean from them.

The checklists and the risk/control tables are somewhat related. A "no" answer on the checklists normally relates to a risk in the risk/control tables.

They are not exactly related as the checklists are designed to go into greater detail to identify potential issues for discussion with your client. When you discuss the checklist results with the client, you should find that the risks you identify from the interviews should closely match the risks described in the risk/control table.

To facilitate any modifications you may require and also to enable electronic workpapers, you can download the risk/control tables and the checklists (audit guide) from the Canaudit web site (*www.canaudit.com/Downloads/ download_register.htm*). After registering, proceed to the E-commerce section and download the files. They are zipped with a password (ice*cream). Enter the password when prompted. As you read the book, you may also want to download some of the tools we use to test security on our clients' E-commerce sites and Internet connections. The password for these files is different (reserve) as they are intended for the participants in our Ultimate Network Penetration Class. You may use them, if you have written permission from your management. Unauthorized use of many of these programs could be a felony. There is a fine line between an auditor or security analyst doing a review of an E-commerce site and a hacker penetrating a network. If you are unsure about using them, please e-mail me and I will go over the basic legal issues with you.

Speaking of legal issues, some of my clients who have used my E-commerce audit approach wonder why I start the review with the legal issues relating to E-commerce. They question why this is even covered. Let me share with you what I share with them. You must ensure that you are conducting business on a strong legal footing. Even though E-commerce is maturing, there are still serious legal issues that have not been codified in some jurisdictions. For example, is an electronic signature acceptance for approval and authorization? To avoid these issues, you must create a contract that enforces your rights before doing E-business with a trading partner. Also, if you want to be able to prosecute when an E-crime occurs, then you will need to ensure that your legal i's are dotted and the t's crossed. You will also have to ensure that your control structure is strong enough to withstand the scrutiny of the defense attorney if you want a prosecution.

As always, I am pleased to answer any questions you may have. Simply e-mail the questions or comments to *Gordon@canaudit.com,* and I will do my best to turn them around quickly. I normally respond to e-mail within 24 hours or less. When I am overseas, the time differences may affect my response time. Lastly, you may need some of our operating system audit guides when performing this audit. We provide checklists for the Windows, UNIX, and Linux environments at no charge. Just e-mail me and I will get them to you as soon as I can.

Now, on to the book. I trust your first E-commerce audit using my methodology will be as successful as it will be interesting.

CHAPTER 1

Introduction

This chapter gives a brief overview of electronic commerce. It will provide you with an understanding of the concepts, some of the earlier implementations, and the risks and benefits of E-commerce. If you already have a good grasp of the concepts, move on to Chapter 2. If not, read on and enjoy.

Electronic commerce is now an acceptable mechanism for conducting business. The early implementations were difficult to use, and faced resistance from the public and from many organizations that were tied to their physical facilities. Banks and retailers had large investments in buildings and infrastructure. They were worried that implementing E-commerce would cause serious financial loss as their physical assets became obsolete. Some did not make the switch to E-commerce and as a result, could not compete effectively. Conversely, many of the early E-businesses, sometimes known as dot.coms, are now dot.gone. They grasped the concepts, created business plans, found funding, and went public. Their share prices shot through the roof, reaching unsustainable levels. They had no earnings, yet they continued to issue more shares. Then the crash came. Fortunes were lost, careers where destroyed, and the lights were turned off on the server farms. (A server farm is a data center that contains many servers in racks, row after row.)

But by this time, the staid, old companies, disparagingly referred to as "bricks and mortar" institutions, had recognized the value of the Internet. They slowly migrated some of their advertising to the web. Their first attempts often looked like online versions of printed brochures. Gradually, they added other services, such as shareholder reports and employment listings. Then came pricing and product information. This quickly led to online ordering, procurement, and customer service systems. Now many of these so-called staid, old companies are fully web integrated and are called "brick and click" organizations. They have faced the Internet challenges, adapted to the changes, and replaced

1

many of their business methods to facilitate web-based customer and vendor transactions.

The successful adaptors have now fully integrated their physical assets with the web assets (often called virtual stores). They have increased sales, and more importantly, they have real bottom-line profits. E-tailing (web-based, consumer-oriented retailing) now accounts for a growing proportion of total retail sales. Today, E-commerce is used to deliver products and services to clients throughout the world. Companies have had to change to keep up with the fast-paced technology boom. As their customer base changed, these companies morphed, changing slow-moving traditional business enterprises into fleet footed, trim, and efficient modern retailers. They are now more adept in reacting to changing customer needs and gauging how best to support those needs. Some customers want to see products in a store before they buy. Others use the web to research the various products and prices, then they go to a store or retail outlet to buy them. Still others prefer to order online, and have the goods or services downloaded or delivered. This last group is fully utilizing E-tailing.

As web-enabled companies evolved, they were able to control costs through effective use of the Internet, which greatly decreased their selling costs and inventory and enhanced their cash flow. They went from selling eight to ten hours per day, five days a week, to offering their products seven days a week, 24 hours a day. Yes, E-commerce has survived the embryonic stage. Of the companies that have changed, most survived; those that could not change withered and were left behind. The present-day bricks and clicks and dot.coms are now stronger, better able to serve their customers, and most importantly, profitable.

E-commerce is now used to automate many mundane, labor-intensive processes, including:

- Product research
- Request for quotes
- Automated customer inquiry
- Electronic order entry
- Outbound and inbound logistics
- Electronic payments
- Customer support and communications

E-commerce has also changed the way business transactions are performed. You can now shop online for insurance, loans, real estate, and even a local dentist. If you want to trade commodities, then the web-enabled businesses are there to execute the trades. If you want to buy a car, you can go online and get quotes from different dealerships. Online banking is now well established. Customers pay bills, transfer money, and monitor their investments online. Tickets for sports and entertainment events are also sold on the web. You can even reserve your theater tickets online and see a view of the stage from the seat you are purchasing.

Yes, E-commerce is here and it is here to stay. There has been some fallout. Some people took jobs with the fast-rising dot.coms, trading salaries for stock options. Fortunes were made, and then lost when the dot.bust occurred. Some people lost their jobs, other people got better jobs. Though this process was hard on many, E-commerce evolved and prospered. In fact, E-commerce is still evolving.

In their haste to get on the web, many organizations took shortcuts. As a result, the required controls often were not put in place. Also, there are many new threats. Hackers can attack an organization at will. New exploits enable them to shut down or seriously disrupt business processes. Viruses and Trojan programs can wreak havoc on a single site or the entire Internet. (A Trojan program is a program that contains unauthorized code. This code may be activated at a specific time or upon the occurrence of a specific event.) Cyber terrorism, the newest threat, is a weapon that can be used against global organizations or a specific country. Why invade a country when you can bring them to their knees electronically? If stock exchanges, banks, phone switches, power, and gas distribution systems were successfully attacked at one time, the impact on the targeted economy would be catastrophic. Entire industries would have to shut down. Networks would be paralyzed. There would be no heat, power, or light. This would be serious indeed for those in colder climates. Ridiculous, you say! Well, we never thought anyone would fly an aircraft into populated buildings. After September 11, we now know that this is a reality. Could there be an electronic 9/11? You bet, so organizations had better be prepared!

My company, Canaudit Inc., is a provider of technical audit and security consulting services. We also provide technical training to the public, our clients, and ISACA (Information Security and Control Association) and IIA (Institute of Internal Auditors) chapters around the world. Our Internet and E-commerce penetration audits have always identified serious control issues. In many cases, we were able to take control of web servers, web applications, and even penetrate the internal networks of our clients. Using simple tools—such as SuperScan, Nessus, and Brutus, just to name a few—many well-known sites have fallen to the Canaudit Strike Force, our team that tests web security. We believe that many E-commerce applications are at serious risk of being compromised, altered, or completely shut down. This can cause serious financial risk, fraud, or unauthorized information disclosure.

The rest of this chapter is devoted to explaining E-commerce, its potential, and a few of the risks. Subsequent chapters will provide you with a step-by-step guide to understanding and securing E-commerce. Each section contains a series of COSO-compliant (Committee of Sponsoring Organizations) checklists and risk control tables that will enable you to perform a security review or audit of your organization's E-commerce installations.

E-COMMERCE RESULTS IN BUSINESS GLOBALIZATION

In the olden days of snail mail and couriers, it could take days or even a week for letters and documents to go from the United States to manufacturers in Singapore. The introduction of the fax machine cut the time, but increased the costs due to slow transmission rates and high international telephone charges. Long documents, such as engineering designs, still had to be couriered. This made it very difficult for global businesses to compete with national businesses and created an artificial barrier to trade and global commerce. With the advent of the Internet, e-mail and documents could literally zing around the world. When in Kuwait recently, I could send e-mail to California, 11 time zones and almost half a world away, in less than two seconds. I was able to order books from Barnes and Noble and have them delivered to my office by the time I returned from my trip.

Business transactions can now be submitted from clients in Dubai, UAE (United Arab Emirates) or Fresno, California. Customers can purchase goods and services any time of day, any day of the week, and in any time zone. They can use their credit card, debit card, or electronic wallets (a secure mechanism to store credit and debit card information on your PC) to make the purchase. Customers can be young teenagers buying electronic games or senior citizens ordering medications. Farmers can order seeds and tools, travelers can order airline tickets, and investors can purchase stock. In most cases, vendor staff are not involved in the ordering process, as the process is fully automated. As a result, there are tremendous gains in productivity, which over time will translate into more profits for web-enabled organizations.

With the advent of electronic procurement and order entry systems, customers can literally be anywhere in the world. It is just as easy to access a web site in India or Argentina as it is in New York or Omaha. Customers can be anywhere and be able to download product lines, item descriptions, and pricing and delivery information. Instead of sending thousands of catalogs to clients around the world, web-enabled businesses can forward the catalogs electronically to the client or have the client download them from a web site. Not only is speed important, but cost is a significant factor as well. It costs no more for 1,000 clients in Detroit to access a catalog than it does for 1,000 clients scattered around the globe to access the same site.

This translates into lower marketing costs. In addition to having your existing clients download the catalog, new clients can find your company on the web and download the catalog and pricing information. This is a very inexpensive way to service existing clients, reach new clients, or expand into other countries. No need to open an office in Moscow; let your Russian customers contact your main E-commerce center. Items can be ordered, pricing can be negotiated, delivery dates specified, and shipping arranged from the facility nearest to the client. It can even be done in their language, provided your web site is truly multinational.

Global E-commerce also applies to other types of businesses. It is just as easy to open an account at Bank of America as it is to open an account with meBANK in Dubai. Accounts can be opened online, money deposited electronically, and funds transferred around the world with the click of a mouse. I can shop around the world in seconds for bank accounts that pay the highest interest, are insured for the entire amount deposited, and are located in a tax-favorable country.

Programmers no longer have to be located in the United States. Why pay $80,000 per year for a programmer in California, when I can hire a programmer in India for $14,000? It does not matter where the employee is located, it only matters that this person can provide me with the code I need, when I need it. Conversely, auditors with special skills located in Simi Valley, California can easily do work on client servers in Dubai or London from the Simi Valley office. While this may sound like a negative item, it can be very positive. We can use highly trained North Americans or Europeans to design complex applications and turn the codification process over to lower cost, yet highly skilled professionals. This enables us to maximize the use of our personnel, yet still be price competitive through internationalizing the programming and support of business applications.

Advertising costs, which used to be measured in the number of brochures or catalogs shipped, pages of print ads purchased, or radio and television ads run, are now measured in terms of web page hits. Using a web page, customers can view products online at a cost to the company of only a few cents or even less. In addition, web pages can be changed immediately to respond to market conditions. Instead of throwing away thousands of outdated brochures, the web page can be altered with a few keystrokes, resulting in a significant savings. Using search engines, new customers can find your products and your site any time, any day, anywhere. Larger organizations often have multilingual sites so that visitors can view the site in their own language.

It has taken several years to get the major brick and click organizations to achieve this objective, but now that they are E-commerce enabled, the incremental costs for E-commerce are actually dropping. Hardware is faster and cheaper. Web applications automate many common business functions. If you are not large enough to host your own E-commerce site, it can be outsourced to an Internet Service Provider (ISP). If you want to have a smaller up-front investment, you can pay by the transaction by outsourcing your E-commerce application to an Application Service Provider (ASP). These providers provide the hardware, software, and the customization, greatly reducing up-front capital costs and ongoing transaction costs.

Another vendor-friendly advantage of E-commerce is automated help and trouble-reporting functions. Customers can access online support and find answers to many of their questions. While this is good for the vendor, I often find that it is not acceptable from the customer standpoint. Have you ever tried the online support from Symantec or Microsoft? It makes you want to whip out your credit card and pay for "human" technical support. That said, many simple problems could be handled through web-based technical support. It is fast, easy, and truly global.

While E-commerce is often considered new, electronic commerce has been around for several decades in other forms. Electronic Data Interchange (EDI) was an early precursor to today's full-blown E-commerce applications. Larger organizations used EDI to automate procurement and many other company-to-company transactions. EDI remains an excellent form of E-commerce, particularly for companies that have very high transaction volumes.

EDI is particularly well suited for computer-to-computer commerce. In an automated EDI ordering application, orders are created by the procurement application. A file of EDI-compliant transactions is prepared and sent to a Value Added Network (VAN) at predetermined times, known as "windows." For example, the window for the widget industry might be from 10 A.M. to 2 P.M., Pacific Standard Time. At 2 P.M., the VAN will consolidate the files and send them out to the various vendors. The vendors will acknowledge the order and provide shipping dates, and so on. The use of a VAN makes EDI affordable for many smaller companies that otherwise could not automate their procurement and order entry functions.

Some companies, particularly in the auto industry, have automated this process so that orders go out instantaneously. They have switched over to fully web-based E-commerce which resides in what is now called the Extranet. The Extranet is physically located outside of a company's internal firewall, but inside their external firewall. In Exhibit 1.1, you will notice that firewall A connects to the Internet through a router. This reduces the likelihood of an Extranet penetration. A second router controls access to the various servers, which are located in the Extranet, and protect data moving from and to the internal network. It is here that authorized customers can place orders and authorized vendors can submit proposals and pricing information. But before they do, they must be authenticated by the applications server. The applications

Exhibit 1.1 The Extranet

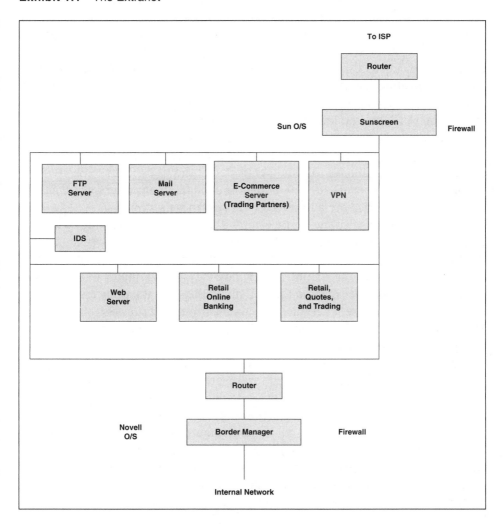

server performs the authentication function and interacts with the procurement server and the order entry server.

There could be many other types of servers in the Extranet. In Exhibit 1.1, there is a router connecting the Extranet to the Internet. Then there is a firewall to protect the Extranet from the Internet and to allow users access to specific devices, depending on what they wish to do. If they want to view information about the company, then they go to the web server. Here they will find information about the services provided, such as online banking or stock trading. If they want investment information about the company, such as financial statements or regulatory filings, then they can go to the file transfer server (FTP server). Here, users can download the information they require. If the FTP server is poorly secured, then hackers, cyber terrorists, or electronic espionage operatives could place a sniffer on the server to sniff passwords or confidential information off the Extranet. They could also load other tools onto the server to compromise security.

If a traveling employee wants to log into the network, they will dial into an Internet Service Provider (ISP) to establish a secure Virtual Private Network connection (VPN) to the internal network. Their session will be encrypted as it travels through the Internet to reduce the likelihood that the messages or data files will be compromised in transit. Before these users can pass into the internal network, they will have to be authenticated at the VPN. Once authenticated, they can enter the network to view e-mail or connect to other servers inside the network, provided they are authorized to access these servers.

An online bank customer or investor will connect to the banking or trading servers. Here they will be authenticated, then given access to their accounts. On the banking server, they may view their balances, pay bills, or transfer money between accounts. On the trading server they may obtain quotes or buy or sell stocks, bonds, and other commodities. Usually these transactions are protected by establishing a secure, encrypted communications path through the Internet. Most applications use Secure Socket Layer (SSL) to ensure privacy and confidentiality of web-enabled transactions.

The early version of E-commerce in the banking industry was Electronic Funds Transfer (EFT). This was used for transferring funds between companies and individuals and Point of Sale (POS) at retailers. It was also used for bank settlements and intercompany transactions. As EFT morphed into E-commerce, a full range of services became available. Home banking is now very popular as it enables bank customers to pay bills online, move funds between accounts, and authorize other types of transactions, such as automated bill payment. Quite frankly, Europe is by far the leader in the use of the Internet and POS to eliminate checks. It will take longer for North Americans to make the transition.

There are several very popular software packages (Quicken, etc.) that enable the home user to automate many of their banking functions. The market still has plenty of room for growth. Eventually, every family will use this software. Just as refrigerators and televisions have become an integral part of the home, so will online banking and financial services.

Some of you may be wondering where the dividing line is between E-commerce and EDI/EFT. Electronic commerce has a much broader scope than EDI. Not only can it handle all types of EDI transactions, but it encompasses Internet- and Extranet-based applications, Interactive Voice Response (IVR), direct debit, and electronic bill payment. With E-commerce, these functions need not be tied to a specific VAN. Using the Internet, business can now be conducted directly with individual consumers (B2C) and consumers can interact with many vendors (C2B). Customers can shop where they choose, search the Internet for the desired product, find the best price, then order it.

In many cases, they must provide their credit or debit card information to the vendor to complete the transaction. From the E-vendor standpoint, this ensures payment is made before delivery, greatly enhancing cash flow. Some consumers still hesitate to buy online, as they are concerned about the security of their credit or debit card. Needless to say, security has been and continues to be addressed. Transactions are protected using encryption and other methods to ensure that critical information is secure as it traverses the Internet on its way to the vendor. However, keep in mind that data still can be compromised in the Extranet or internal network.

Not only does payment before delivery enhance cash flow, but it can reduce currency exchange losses (or gains). If I wish to purchase something in France from the United States, I may pay with my credit card in Euros. Visa will automatically convert this into dollars for me. Because this happens immediately, the buyer and seller can complete the transaction right away. Not only are exchange losses minimized, but the transaction can be conducted without buying any special equipment. This makes it simple for small businesses to access the global marketplace using E-commerce.

While it is both easy and cost effective for any business to establish a global E-commerce capability, there are serious security issues that must be resolved. Encryption is used to secure most financial transactions. I take issue primarily with authentication and the security of the web servers themselves. Many of our clients think they are safe because they have a firewall. As you will find out later in the book, there are many ways to bypass the firewall and get at data on Extranet servers and possibly in the internal network.

When it comes to Internet shopping, many North Americans think that they can only buy from companies in their country. The Europeans have been using trans-border shopping for years. Since most E-tailers use the electronic warehouse concept, the clients need not even know where the product is located. The electronic mall is very similar to a real department store, except it is not crowded and there are no lines at the checkout counter. Courier services such as UPS, FedEx, Airborne Express, and others make the world a small place indeed. About a month before I wrote this chapter, I was E-shopping at a security site in New Zealand. I placed my order, and in three days the goods were in my office. When I had a problem with one of the devices, I e-mailed the company, they authorized a return, and sent me a new item.

Global shopping is also a good way to get the lowest price, but there is a risk. When ordering, be careful that you are not ordering "gray market goods."

Most major companies license their distributors by country. This enables a large electronics firm to offer products at market prices within each country or region. If you were to order a DVD player from India, you would get a cheaper price. However, it may not be legal to import it into your country. Also, if the product needs to be serviced, the warranty may not be honored.

To summarize, companies like to do business globally on the Internet. It reduces their dependence on any one market. It enables them to offer products at lower costs. They may be able to bypass distributor issues and sell directly to the customer. They also may be able to avoid paying commissions. In addition, they do not have to warehouse their goods. The product can be shipped directly from the manufacturing site or an outsourced manufacturing site using couriers.

With E-commerce, customers have a broader choice of products and pricing; they are not limited to one region or country. They can order and pay online and track the goods throughout the delivery process. Software can be downloaded immediately, eliminating the need to ship CD-ROMs and manuals. Customer assistance and help desks are online 24 hours a day, seven days a week, providing service and assistance to customers. And best of all, in some countries, there are no sales taxes on goods purchased on the Internet.

Despite all the positives, there is a downside. Hackers can attack web sites at will from anywhere in the world. They can deface web pages, knock a site down with a Denial of Service (DoS) attack, or penetrate the web servers. In many cases, they can download credit card and other sensitive information to use in frauds or simply to embarrass an organization. They can also plant viruses and Trojan programs on the machines, install back doors, and steal client passwords. As you can see, global E-commerce has risks as well as benefits. As you read subsequent chapters, you will learn more about the specific risks and how to mitigate risk through a series of structured controls. You will also learn how to test your site, just as hackers do, enabling you to implement preemptive security (finding the holes and fixing them before hackers can exploit the weaknesses).

This book is designed to provide you with a structured, layered approach to controlling and securing your organization's E-commerce activities. Each of the chapters covers a separate component of E-commerce to provide you with an understanding of the risks and the controls required to mitigate the risks. Using the checklists and risk/control matrices provided in each chapter, you will be able to conduct your audit or security review quickly and efficiently. The checklists, found at the end of each chapter, have been consolidated into an audit guide. The risk/control matrices have been consolidated into a risk assessment guide. Both of these documents are available in electronic form on the attached on the Canaudit web site, *www.canaudit.com*. In addition, much of the software mentioned in this book can also be found on the web site.

CHAPTER 2

Legal Issues Related to E-Commerce

In this chapter we will address the legal issues related to E-commerce. Many of you may wonder why I choose to start here, instead of covering the technical issues first. The answer is simple. Once we move into an electronic environment, many of the laws that have historically governed business transactions no longer apply. The Uniform Commercial Code (UCC) does not cover electronic documents. Fortunately, new legislation now makes electronic signatures acceptable. Even so, there still is not enough case law to establish the legal guidelines required to provide the sound legal basis that senior executives need.

While the UCC does not specifically cover E-commerce, the United Nations Model Law on Commerce does. The UN Commission on International Trade Law (UNCITRAL) has created a model law for International electronic trading. This is one of the finest pieces of business legislation ever passed. The model law now covers many of the topics related to E-commerce including the Model Law on Electronic Commerce and the Model Law on Electronic Signatures. You can visit their web site at *www.uncitral.org/en-index.htm* for specific information on the Model laws, case law, adopted text for E-trading, and the like.

Because many countries still have not adopted the Model Law, contract law can make up for the deficiencies in the Uniform Commercial Code and case law. Therefore, it is very important to create a contract that protects your organization when entering into an electronic relationship with your trading partners. The concept of mutual consent and definite terms constitutes offer and acceptance. From your business law courses, you will probably remember that for a contract to be valid, there must be an offer, acceptance of the offer, and legal consideration (money or value for value). The gray area with electronic transactions is the issue of human interaction in the transaction. When I visit a client

11

and sign a deal, there is human interaction; it is easy to demonstrate that there is a contract. Telephone transactions are also accepted as legitimate because of the immediate two-way communication between the parties. A fax is accepted as a valid transaction because there is a paper trail and a physical signature (even if it is telecommunicated). If there are to be E-commerce transactions, then there needs to be an E-commerce contract.

Contract law can also assist us by defining notification and what constitutes notification. How do we legally advise electronic business partners of critical business communications? Under the mailbox rule, notification is considered given when the notice is placed in the mail, unless another mechanism to define notification is specified in the contract. This rule is valid in the United States and many other countries. The offerer is bound by an acceptance, provided it is placed in the mail on or before the required date. The offerer is bound even if they did not receive the letter or contract. Placing the letter in the mail establishes the date for official notification because that is when the party mailing the item clearly intended the transaction to be considered final. This is the reason many people have the post office provide a receipt when mailing tax returns and other important, date-sensitive documents.

In the E-commerce world there are no physical mailboxes. As a result, there must be a contractual date and a contract to govern the terms of the agreement. Can a company be held liable if it did not receive an order because of an ISP or server failure? Yes, they can if there is a contract that specifies that the seller is required to deliver when the buyer sends the e-mail. While this may be the point in time that the contract is solidified, in point of fact, there is no proof that the contract exists. That is why many contracts specify that the order is valid when the other party has confirmed it. The buyer must contact the seller if he or she does not receive a confirmation of the order within a prespecified time frame. This puts the onus back on the originator of the transaction and is quite different from the mailbox rule.

Many of us have purchased software on the Internet. I love doing this because I can get the latest version of the software and download it in minutes. It saves me having to find a store that sells it, driving to the store, purchasing the item, and loading the CD-ROM. From a legal standpoint, when I buy a physical copy of the software, I am bound by the license agreement just by opening the package. This fact may be displayed on the outside of the package or in the license agreement that comes with the package. But when I download software from the Internet, there is no seal on the box. In fact, there is no box. That is why you normally have to click on the "I ACCEPT" box before the software will download. Most people I know click on this right away. They never read the contract that precedes this button. This can be very dangerous, as you may be agreeing to something that you ordinarily would not. For instance, if you were to subscribe to a free e-mail service, you might find that the service has the right to copyright or patent any item that is transmitted through their service. Or, you might discover that they have the right to publish your transmission and use your name. In these cases, it is quite possible that the ISP would in fact own the material in question.

Now some of you will read this and say that there was offer and acceptance, but no consideration or value was exchanged. But in fact there was. You were given the ability to send and receive e-mail. An ISP may charge $15 or $20 per month for this service, which establishes the value. There was a value for value exchange. Be careful to read the contract before you accept the terms. The concept of caveat emptor (let the buyer beware) is often forgotten in the E-business world. Most people are very trusting and are bored by contracts. One thing I like to keep in mind is that if I click on "I ACCEPT," I may be granting someone the right to drain my bank account. By reminding myself of this, I find I make the better choice and read the contract.

In addition to reading the contract, you should ensure that there is always a confirmation of any order. Some electronic trading partners use mirroring of the offer and the acceptance. Mirroring is the communication of the offer to a party and the other party sending it back to the originating party. This demonstrates that they received it correctly and that this is a transaction history to support the offer and acceptance (sometimes called an audit trail). It also solidifies the existence of a contract. I sent my offer to you. You sent it back to me indicating that you received it. You then sent an acceptance. I received it and mirrored it back to you, indicating that I received your acceptance. Another term for mirroring is "echo back." You may see or hear both terms in your audit or security review of E-commerce.

Outdated legislation can also create problems in many jurisdictions. For instance, the Statute of Frauds requires "some note or memorandum in writing signed by the parties" to have an enforceable contract if the value of the goods is over $500. Just what satisfies "in writing" is subject to interpretation. Clearly, printing, typewriting, or any other "intentional reduction to tangible form" is acceptable. Under new E-commerce laws, mirroring and digital signatures should satisfy this requirement, once there is a test case. However, no one is rushing into court to establish the precedent. Remember that we still have to prove that the digital signature was sent. It is not enough to say, "I sent it on May 15. It is in my sent items box."

How do we deal with transactions that are completely automated? An agent can bind an insurance company without the prior knowledge of the insurance company. Will the courts accept electronic agents, such as software programs? Under old style laws, transactions could be submitted in person or by phone because it was clear that there was a transaction and a negotiation process between two humans. Once we enter the electronic realm, a human is not involved in the ordering process; hence there may not be a discernible offer and acceptance by humans. Rather than take a risk that the electronic agents will be rejected, an electronic contract is used to ensure that the software agent is a recognized process and that the transaction is binding.

E-COMMERCE IN THE COURTROOM

Much of the law relating to electronic commerce is untested. Business is going where no lawyer has gone before. Eventually, the law will catch up; however, from a business standpoint we cannot wait. In a digital world, what constitutes evidence in court? Mirroring and echo back should be sufficient. Clicking on the I ACCEPT button should suffice. But if you never read the contract before you accepted it, what jury is going to rule in your favor? Conversely, if you can prove that the contract was confusing and difficult to understand, then a jury may agree with you. Therefore, it is up to the customer to read and accept the contract and up to the vendor to ensure that the contract is clear, concise, and straightforward.

Another thing to consider is the effect of a court trial in an E-commerce case. Your organization's control structure, or lack thereof, could lead to public embarrassment. If data is not stored with integrity then it is not acceptable as evidence. Based on this premise, if your controls are poor, the other party could have your electronic documentation ruled inadmissible. Password crackers and trust relationships could be used to establish that your systems are not secure, and the transactions in question may therefore be nullified.

Let me explain this a little further. Most people have heard stories of hackers penetrating a corporate network and damaging business systems. If you have poor controls, such as an account without a password, a hacker can gain access to the system. There are well-known exploits to gain access to the system at the administrator or root level, granting the hacker the ability to create or delete accounts or files. There are many password crackers on the Internet, and virtually anyone has access to these tools. When we do our penetration audits, most passwords crack within a few minutes. Once we have "smartened" our dictionary with passwords that are unique to a specific target, we can crack passwords in seconds. Imagine the impact to your business when your passwords are being cracked in a courtroom—hundreds of passwords in just a few minutes! Obviously, this could jeopardize your case.

It is also possible that the plaintiff's attorney could use a demon dialer to penetrate your network by finding a poorly secured modem. They can do this with the court's permission. If they succeed in penetrating your network and accessing confidential data, will your digital records be considered to have integrity? Not a chance! The plaintiff's attorney could also request copies of past audit and security reports during the discovery process. If the application was audited, found to have poor controls, and those controls were not corrected, then it is possible that a jury of our peers could be convinced that the transaction, database, and operating system logs cannot be relied upon to ensure the integrity of the data. Again, a good lawyer will be able to show that the evidence could be tainted. Exhibit 2.1 provides some password files that we cracked (in the examples, the passwords all cracked within 15 seconds).

Exhibit 2.1   Cracked Password Files

Account	Password	User Id	Group Id
checkfsys	(blank)	0	0
mapdiag	(blank)	0	3
mapperb	(blank)	20001	100
mapperc	(blank)	20001	100
mapperd	(blank)	20010	100
mapsa	(blank)	0	100
mlsadmin	(blank)	0	1
mountfsys	(blank)	0	0
mri	(blank)	20004	100
mtty	(blank)	20003	100
ncrmusr	(blank)	102	1004
setup	(blank)	0	0
slip	(blank)	72	2
sync	(blank)	67	1
umountfsys	(blank)	0	0
sclocal	(blank)	99	99
console	console	23333	1
lmt	lmt	9489	893
mmis	mmis	20753	753
operator	operator	0	1
psdxfer	psdxfer	13800	456
visitor	visitor	12563	303
zortec	zortec	20200	200
tsreorg	tsreorg	106	20
Batch_remote	new	-10396	1
PElogin	new	-10397	1
ah	new	1727	891
ally	new	-10402	1007
amc	new	1650	625
ats	new	7549	692

(continues)

Exhibit 2.1   Cracked Password Files *(Continued)*

Account	Password	User Id	Group Id
atsna	new	-10412	894
bam	new	-10095	625
bas	new	4728	625
bcs	new	1457	880
beebe	new	8693	893
brb2798	new	2798	1020
brb	sherry1	-25660	503
cap	new	4315	893
cis132	new	20014	503
cis	new	21503	503
cke	new	8861	870
ckk	chris	1982	893
cld	daniel	3927	100
clf	forte1	1868	625
cmrtst	jpl	12455	1003
crg	new	8793	625
css	new	10003	1003
cth	new	-26703	625
cwh3752	new	3752	1020
daf	new	3896	625
dais	new	30463	1002
das73	new	8094	650
das	debbie1	4295	880
davox	new	17549	503
dda	new	3983	360
dej	new	9077	753
der	new	2010	750
dertst	new	21010	1003
dew881	new	30335	503
dkc	new	1951	802
dks	new	1546	802
dlm	new	-10398	302
dls	stock1	2039	802
dmm	new	8292	625

The accounts with a user ID of zero are root-empowered. The account we used to penetrate this system was the same account I found on a similar audit over 25 years ago: operator with a password of operator. Clearly, some organizations are control adverse and will fair poorly if they need to prosecute an E-commerce fraud or are sued for disclosure of confidential customer information.

During a trial, the chain of custody could also be used against you. Data must be stored with integrity and be safe from tampering if you want to use it in a legal proceeding. To be accepted into its evidence you must establish that:

- The transaction was performed in a secure manner.
- The record is accurate.
- The record was not altered.
- The hardware, software, and network connections are secure and reliable.

If you cannot provide this proof, then U.S. Federal Rule of Evidence 901(9) can be used against you. From the results of Canaudit's penetration audits and security reviews, I can safely state that most organizations will not be able to prove these four requirements and hence the opposition would likely win. To avoid this, major banks and financial institutions print out, microfilm, or microfiche transactions daily and store them in a locked warehouse. A court accepts this as an original document from a rules of evidence standpoint. When I discussed this with an attorney, he mentioned that if the documents are printed, fiched, or microfilmed, they would likely be deemed to be correct even though the electronic data demonstrates that they are wrong.

The reason is that you must be able to prove that the data is accurate, stored with integrity, has not been altered, and there is strong and effective security over the data. In some cases, the incorrect paper document would be accepted and the correct digital data would be rejected due to the lack of a strong internal control structure.

As I travel around giving lectures, a question I am often asked is: "If electronic controls are so bad, why do we not hear of more cases of E-fraud?" The answer is quite simple. If an organization's control structure would not hold up to scrutiny in court, there is no point in prosecuting. As a result, many electronic frauds are simply written off; controls are improved for a while and then business goes back to normal. Also, court proceedings are public. The threat of public disclosure of the company's control weaknesses could certainly convince some executives not to prosecute. Just think of the impact a major fraud could have on the stock price! From an executive standpoint, it may be better to take the hit as an extraordinary item and move on.

Let me emphasize here that prevention is very important. Strong controls and an aggressive audit department, coupled with regular reviews, can ensure that an organization's E-commerce application is properly protected. A point I often make in my E-commerce audit reports is that the company may not be able to prosecute a fraud or recover the funds unless they have strong internal controls. The Gram Leach Bliley legislation requires that customer information be protected. When this law was passed, across the board there was a temporary increase on management's part to improve internal controls. Now that the Sarbanes-Oxley Act has passed, executives are required to sign off on their internal control structures. The effective use of these acts over time can lead to a significant improvement in controls and ensure that management is motivated to correct control weaknesses when they are discovered.

Before leaving this topic, let's examine another issue with regard to audit reports. Management comments or responses are often part of the audit reporting process. At Canaudit, we believe that it is now best to leave management comments out of the audit report. Just imagine how a jury might react to seeing the following management comment in an audit report: "While we agree with the internal auditor, at this time, there is no money in the budget to correct the problem." This would look very foolish indeed if the audit issue had been mentioned in several reports spanning many years, especially during times when the company reported record earnings. The jurors may ask, "If there are record earnings, why is there no money in the budget?"

Another comment that potentially could be very embarrassing would be, "We do not perceive that the issue reported by the internal auditor poses a significant risk." The lawyers would have a field day with that comment. Therefore, keep in mind while reviewing the control structure of an E-commerce application that the audit report could end up as evidence in a civil suit. There is no need to give the plaintiff's attorney any more ammunition that could be used to substantiate that the company was negligent. This could result in punitive damages of up to three times the actual loss involved.

If the plaintiff can demonstrate that management was advised of the risk, understood the risk, and chose not to address the risk, management could be deemed negligent should the risk occur. If they are negligent and the organization loses the case, they could be liable for treble damages. In short, remove the management comments or responses from the audit reports. Instead, prioritize the items based on risk. This demonstrates that the items were known and that they may or will be addressed. If an incident occurs, management can rightly say that they intended to correct the problem, however the situation happened before they could correct it. Yes, it is semantics, but isn't that what happens in a courtroom?

Let's use a funds transfer application as an example. Suppose a fraudulent wire transfer is made from a customer's account. In funds transfer agreements, the requirement for security rests (generally) with the customer unless the bank fails to use appropriate security procedures and the customer can prove that security was compromised. If so, the bank may lose the case, as their internal controls must have broken down. Another way the customer can win is if the bank has no facility for securing the transactions.

To protect themselves, banks often offer several forms of authentication including digital certificates and digital signatures, fax back confirmations, or a simple telephone conversation. Surprisingly, my experience demonstrates that the customer usually accepts the simplest form of security, which is often ineffective. Then, when there is a problem, the bank can say that they advised the client to use strong authentication, however the client declined, and here is the form signed by the client indicating they declined the appropriate security.

To conclude this section, it is very important that strong controls be in place in an E-commerce environment and that these controls be audited on a regular basis. Management should be responsive to correcting audit issues and encourage a strong control environment.

LEGAL AGREEMENTS IN SUPPORT OF E-COMMERCE

Legal agreements are necessary because in many jurisdictions the law does not specifically recognize electronic commerce. We now have several laws in the United States that facilitate electronic commerce. Even so, it is better to have a good contract to ensure that the terms and conditions in a trading partner relationship are understood and are enforceable.

Signatures and writings are a key point of contract law. Electronic signatures are now acceptable in many jurisdictions. In the past, a proper signature on paper was required to sign a contract. Next, a telegram also became acceptable. A facsimile, or fax, as we now call it, came next. Finally electronic signatures are now accepted for most contracts.

One of the last bastions of paper transactions was the IRS. For years they did not accept electronic returns. Now they mail out a personal identification number to enable those who want to file electronically to do so. By placing this number on the electronic form, it is considered to be confirmation that the taxpayer has submitted the return and is certifying that the return is correct.

Contracts are often required to ensure electronic transactions are enforceable. This is particularly true for large value transactions. Organizations that agree to do business with each other are called trading partners. You may see the term B2B used in conjunction with electronic trading partners, which stands for business to business. In a B2B relationship, the trading partners normally have a trading partner agreement to outline the specific terms and conditions of their business relationship. There are different types of contracts depending on the type of products and services offered. One type of agreement is for the electronic procurement of goods and services. For example, auto manufacturers have automated most of their purchase transactions. By removing the human interface from the ordering process, they are able to significantly reduce labor costs. In addition to agreements for purchases and sales, there are other types of trading partner agreements. These include contracts for Internet service providers, carrier contracts with the various phone companies (where the customer and phone company negotiate a contract specifying the services provided, the fees, and terms and conditions relating to the services) and third party contracts with Internet retailers who may market your products.

If there is no Trading Partner Agreement (TPA), issues that could have a significant financial impact must be resolved through the legal system at great cost. Trading partner agreements avoid many of the legal pitfalls by creating a binding contract that is enforceable. Some of the items that should be included in a TPA are contained in Exhibit 2.2.

Exhibit 2.2 Contracting Requirements for Trading Partner Agreements

Item	Meaning
Acceptance	Description of what constitutes a legal acceptance and binding obligation.
Binding obligations	This specifies that both trading partners agree that electronic commerce transactions are binding obligations and can be enforced.
Business continuance	This documents the business continuance and disaster preparedness requirements of the Value Added Network (VAN).
Confidentiality	This defines what information is public and what information is confidential. It also includes exceptions to confidentiality, such as for use in a legal proceeding.
Intent to contract	This is used to indicate that the parties are entering into a contract for electronic commerce and that the computer transactions between them are valid and binding.
Legal notice	This specifies how legal notices are to be delivered, either in writing or electronically (or both).
Liability	The liability of each trading partner is specified.
Message integrity	This specifies that it is the receiving party's responsibility to check that the message was received correctly and is usable. It should also specify the actions to be taken when corrupted messages are received.

Exhibit 2.2   Contracting Requirements for Trading Partner
Agreements *(Continued)*

Item	Meaning
Method of communicating transactions	This identifies the communications alternatives that will be used by the trading partners to send transactions. It can include dialed and leased connections as well as the VAN or the Internet.
Offer	This is a description of what constitutes an offer.
Receipt	A definition of what constitutes receipt of goods. FOB (Free on Board) our plant means shipping paid by customer. FOB your door means shipping paid by vendor.
Related costs	This specifies that each partner will pay their own costs relating to the trading partner arrangement.
Resolution of disputes	This defines the process for resolving disputes. Some contracts may specify litigation, others may specify arbitration.
Retention	The requirements for data retention are specified. Ensure that you conform to this, as the ability to provide a transaction in court may be a deciding factor in litigation.
Security	This defines each partner's responsibility for security and the need to provide notification of a security breach to other trading partners.
Signature issues	This specifies that electronic signatures are acceptable in place of a written signature.

Another type of trading partner agreement is for a Value Added Network (VAN). These networks provide services to E-businesses such as EDI and processing of E-commerce transactions. By combining network access with some application processing, VANs can help an organization in the following ways:

- VANs provide cheaper connections than a direct connection to each trading partner.
- VANs may provide faster service than dial-up connections.

- VANs are easier to manage and can handle the following services:
  - Store and forward
  - Transcription services
  - Communications services

An Application Service Provider is even better than a VAN for companies that want to provide E-commerce solutions to their trading partners, but do not want the costs and overhead related to building and maintaining their own E-commerce software. The ASP hosts the web site for the client and processes the transactions. To the customer, it looks like the organization is providing the service—they need not know that an ASP is actually doing the job.

As with trading partners, there should be a contract for VANs and ASPs. Be careful that you do not accept the standard contract, as it is designed to protect the service provider, not the organization using their services. Exhibit 2.3 provides some of the key points that should be included in the contract.

Exhibit 2.3   Contracting Requirements for Value Added Networks and Application Service Providers

Item	Meaning
Business continuance	This documents the business continuance and disaster preparedness requirements of the VAN or ASP.
Contract termination	This specifies the contract termination conditions including required notice and responsibilities of each party for transferring data to another VAN or ASP or a centralized site.
Data retention	This specifies the time frame that the VAN or ASP will retain customer data. This is useful as an offsite backup for electronic commerce transactions.
Help and support	This defines the help desk hours and the types of services offered. An 800 number should be specified.
Liability	The mutual liabilities for the trading partner and the VAN or ASP are specified.
Offered services	This describes the services offered under the contract, the pricing, and any surcharges that apply.

Exhibit 2.3   Contracting Requirements for Value Added Networks and
Application Service Providers *(Continued)*

Item	Meaning
Ownership of customer data	This is a critical point. Already several VANs have sold customer information. Therefore title to customer data should be clearly specified. Also, the VAN or ASP should not be able to sell or use customer information.
Resolution of disputes	This defines the process for resolving disputes. Some contracts may specify litigation, others may specify arbitration.
Right to audit	The trading partner should have the right to a third-party audit report and to conduct audits in addition to the third-party report. Note: When reviewing an SAS 70 report, remember to identify the controls that are absent. These reports normally talk about the controls that are present, not the controls that are missing.
Security	This outlines the security to be used for your transactions and also the types of access that your firm is authorized to use. It should also define unauthorized access and the measures to be taken if unauthorized access is detected.
Service levels	This defines the acceptable service level. For instance, 99.5 percent of the time, a transaction will be forwarded within 5 minutes of receipt. Also, a provision for outages and outage-related costs could be included here.
Time frame	This defines the cut-off times for transactions and also the hours that services are available.

RISK/CONTROL TABLE

Now that we have covered many of the issues, here are some sample risk control tables that will assist you in performing your first review or audit of an E-commerce application. You should review the tables and modify them to suit your environment.

Risk	Control	Status
Many organizations are conducting business electronically without considering the legal issues surrounding electronic commerce.	The organization should fully investigate the legal ramifications of electronic commerce before implementing electronic commerce, even on a test basis.	
The Uniform Commercial Code and the U.S. Statute of Frauds do not specifically recognize electronic commerce. For instance, the Statute of Frauds requires "some note or memorandum in writing signed by the parties" to constitute an enforceable contract. As a result, the organization may not be paid for sales or shipments or may not be able to seek damages for breach of contract.	A trading partner agreement is required to establish the contractual obligations of the business partners. A law firm that specializes in electronic commerce should prepare the contracts.	
Notification of the acceptance of an offer need not be received to create a valid contract. As a result, the organization may be contractually obligated even though they do not receive the notification of acceptance. The organization could be liable for penalties, damages, and/or legal costs.	The trading partner agreement should address the issue of notification and acceptance of an offer. It should state that an offer is not considered accepted until it is "mirrored" or "echoed back" from the vendor.	

Risk	Control	Status
If transactions are completely automated, a claim could be made that no one accepted the contract.	In this case, the trading partner agreement should contain a phrase that binds the obligations of both parties even if electronic agents are used to process the transaction.	
For evidence to be acceptable in court, the Rules of Evidence must be followed. In addition, the chain of custody must be maintained in a secure manner. If your organization's controls do not protect the data from alteration, deletion, or the creation of unauthorized transactions, then U.S. Federal Rule of Evidence 901 (9) can be used against you. Based on our audits, many of our clients could not prove that they stored the data with integrity and that the chain of evidence was preserved.	Many of the controls that auditors have pushed for in the past are now essential. Restricting programmer access to data, strong logical controls, R factor balancing, and other techniques are required to ensure that your data will be acceptable in court.	
Without proper controls in place, the organization will be unable to successfully prosecute a fraud. A smart crook may be able to keep the money and escape prosecution because your organization does not want a shoddy control structure presented in court.	The control structure for electronic transactions should be reviewed using the higher standard required for Federal Rules of Evidence and the chain of evidence. This control structure should be well documented, tested using electronic espionage techniques, and certified. If you cannot maintain the required control structure, then the transactions should be printed daily and stored in an offsite warehouse. Printed data is considered "original" by the legal system.	

(continues)

Risk	Control	Status
A failure to review the bank contract could result in a serious financial exposure, should a fraud or defalcation occur.	Review the bank funds transfer contract to ensure that the security offered by the bank is implemented. In addition, ensure that the organization can prove the existence of a strong internal control structure.	
An ASP or VAN may not have adequate controls. As a result, transactions could be lost, altered, or seriously delayed.	Insist on a copy of the ASP's or VAN's third-party review. In addition, your organization should have the right to audit items not covered in the third-party review. Ensure the ASP or VAN has a tested business continuance and disaster preparedness plan. In addition, you may want to participate in testing of the plan.	
The VAN's contract usually places all risk on the customer. As a result, it is difficult to receive restitution when the VAN has a serious technical problem or acts in an inappropriate manner.	Negotiate a strong VAN agreement using a law firm that specializes in electronic commerce.	

AUDIT CHECKLIST

I have developed a series of checklists that Canaudit uses to perform E-commerce audits. These can be found at the end of the chapters and should be given to the client to complete several weeks before the fieldwork for the audit or review begins.

No.	Question	Yes	No	WP XREF	REP XREF
1.	**Did the organization fully investigate the legal ramifications of electronic commerce?**				
	a. Was the legal department involved?				
	b. Was a legal expert with strong experience in electronic commerce used to assist in this effort?				
2.	**Is there a trading partner agreement for each of the trading partners you do business with?**				
	a. Is it formalized?				
	b. Does it protect your rights?				
3.	**Does the trading partner agreement cover the following issues:**				
	a. Acceptance?				
	b. Binding obligations?				
	c. Confidentiality?				
	d. Intent to contract?				
	e. Legal notice?				
	f. Liability?				
	g. Message integrity?				
	h. Method of communicating transactions?				
	i. Offer?				
	j. Receipt?				

(continues)

No.	Question	Yes	No	WP XREF	REP XREF
	k. Related costs?				
	l. Resolution of disputes?				
	m. Retention?				
	n. Security?				
	o. Signature issues?				
4.	**Is a mirrored transaction (or echo back) used to confirm the acceptance of an offer?**				
5.	**Is there a provision in the contract to ensure that completely automated transactions are binding?**				
6.	**Is the control structure of the electronic commerce application strong enough to meet the Rules of Evidence and chain of custody requirements?**				
	a. Are the controls documented?				
	b. Have they been tested?				
	c. Has a third party certified the controls?				
7.	**Do the application controls include the following minimum standard of control:**				
	a. Authorization?				
	b. Authentication?				
	c. Backup and recovery?				
	d. Business continuance?				
	e. Database integrity?				
	f. Data change management?				
	g. Network security and integrity?				
	h. Operating system integrity?				

No.	Question	Yes	No	WP XREF	REP XREF
	i. Program change management?				
	j. Restricted access for programmers?				
	k. Secure custody?				
	l. Separation of duties?				
	n. Sophisticated balancing techniques?				
	o. Storage integrity?				
8.	**Has the operating system hosting the electronic commerce application been audited?**				
	a. Do the operating system controls currently installed ensure a secure environment?				
	b. Has the operating system hosting the application been penetration tested?				
9.	**Has the network supporting the electronic commerce application been audited?**				
	a. Is the network considered secure?				
	b. Has the network been penetration tested?				
10.	**Is the organization confident that the controls over their applications are sufficient to withstand the scrutiny of a trial lawyer in a criminal prosecution?**				
	a. If not, are transactions printed out daily and stored offsite so that they will be considered "original" documents?				
11.	**Has the bank's funds transfer agreement been reviewed to ensure that the organization is protected?**				
	a. Is the highest level of security offered by the bank used for communicating funds transfer information?				

(continues)

No.	Question	Yes	No	WP XREF	REP XREF
	b. Has the security of the host operating system and network been reviewed?				
	c. Is the bank connection secure?				
	d. Would the control structure for the funds transfer system stand up well in court?				
12.	**Is there a legal agreement with the ASP or VAN?**				
13.	**Does the ASP or VAN contract include the following items?**				
	a. Business continuance?				
	b. Contract termination?				
	c. Data retention?				
	d. Help and support?				
	e. Liability?				
	f. Offered services?				
	g. Ownership and use of data?				
	h. Resolution of disputes?				
	i. Right to audit?				
	j. Security?				
	k. Service levels?				
	l. Time frame for transaction cutoff?				
14.	**Are you confident in the control structure of the electronic commerce application?**				
15.	**Are you confident in the controls over the hosting operating systems and network?**				

CHAPTER 3

Information Security: Overview

Basic information security is available in many other publications. However, some of these items need to be covered again, both as a refresher for those who are already familiar with basic information controls and to apply these controls to the E-commerce environment. Physical security controls, which I generally consider to be the old school general controls review, is actually very important in the E-commerce environment. In many penetration and network audits, web servers have been found to be very insecure. Exhibits 3.1 and 3.2 are pictures of real web servers found during audits.

Exhibit 3.1   Picture of a Web Server

Exhibit 3.2 Poorly Positioned S/390 Machine

In Exhibit 3.1, notice the scotch bottle in the tall white tube in front of the server, the soda cans, and the bottle of water. This was the most astonishing alcohol–server combination in my 29 years of auditing.

Exhibit 3.2 is an S/390. In addition to performing web-based functions, it is also used as a desk.

While these pictures are unusual, we have found several other physical security issues. For example, a Canaudit staff member found a vent in a door that was not secured. He simply crawled through the vent and had complete access to the network equipment. All he had to do was set up a wireless access point in the network room and he could then sit in a hotel across the street and monitor web activity, copy client information, compromise credit cards, and view confidential financial information.

Given pictures and stories such as these, good physical security is still a very necessary "best practice" in an E-commerce environment. This means that the data center housing the E-commerce site must be physically secure. Doors should be locked. Access should be restricted by keycard, biometrics, or other form of automated access device. In a very high-risk environment, such as a large retail or financial web business, there also should be an effective process to monitor access and prevent piggy-backing. Piggy-backing occurs when an authorized person swipes a keycard in the key station and a second person sneaks behind the first person, but does not swipe his or her card to enter.

If your E-business servers are outsourced, the need for physical security increases rather than decreases. Your E-business may be sharing a server, file system, or databases with other clients. While many of my clients rely on an SAS 70 report from a "Big Four" CPA firm, you should retain the right to audit the facility. (Statement of Audit Standards (SAS) 70 is an independent external audit of a service provider. It is intended to give the provider's clients assurance that controls are in place.) At least once a year, plan on performing a physical inspection of the facility.

Another security issue that must be considered is control over staff and contractors. Several of our clients have experienced frauds or theft of customer information for use in identity theft. Many of our clients have secured the clients' access from the Internet using a firewall, yet the internal network is subject to attack by staff and contractors on the inside who have access to the E-commerce processing assets.

A common flaw in judgment is often made when management assumes that their employees and contractors are all honest. At the time of this writing, a major client had a senior vice president "go bad." He was employed by one company, but selling confidential information to a competitor for more money than he was getting from his employer. He got caught by accident during our audit. When we were reviewing network traffic, we found an unusually large amount of data being transmitted from his machine. When we reviewed the files on his machine and his e-mail, we found that he was indeed transferring data to a competitor. Now if he was smart, he would have set up a wireless access point in a relatively public area of the company and let the competitor take the files off the E-commerce server themselves while parked in the adjacent parking structure. Neat, clean, and no way to get caught!

In another case, we had a banking client that had a large auto-lending portfolio. Dealers would enter data online or send in the applications by fax. The faxed applications were keyed by low-level contract employees. In this case, the contract data entry person was not a low-level individual at all. He had a masters degree in computer science. He was keying the data, but then he was using an unauthorized modem to send the data to his home computer. He and some friends were gathering this information so it could be used in identity theft. We were fortunate to catch them in the early stages of their project during our demon dial test to identify unauthorized and poorly protected modems. They had not yet used any of the stolen identities, so our timing was excellent.

Business continuance and disaster preparedness is also very important in an E-commerce environment. If a customer wants to sell stock in the early stages of a market downturn and is unable to do so, then the broker may be held civilly responsible for any loss. A few years ago, a major financial services firm did indeed have a problem of this nature. Rather than waiting to be sued, they voluntarily identified clients who were affected by the outage, determined their actual loss, and reimbursed them. Not many companies would do this without a legal suit being filed. They paid out millions of dollars in order to protect their E-commerce business.

I often use this case to demonstrate that business continuance is a very important part of E-commerce. While many auditors and IT professionals are still working on disaster recovery plans, I have focused my clients on business continuance. In my mind, there must be enough redundancy to ensure that critical E-commerce functions never fail. If a data center is lost in an earthquake or terrorist event, then processing should "fail over" (transfer upon failure) to another location. Larger companies will need to have multiple sites where the data and programs are mirrored. If a terrorist group decided to attack a major corporation, it is possible that they could destroy one, two, or even three data centers.

Mirroring data and programs to several locations may seem expensive at first. However, in addition to business continuance, it also provides the ability to improve performance and reduce contention. When customer activity on the east coast is very high and transaction processing time degrades, a server on the west coast could be used to process the transaction. This type of load balancing is a very effective side benefit to business continuance. By combining the two functions, cost justification of multiple, mirrored processing sites may be easier.

Another issue that is of concern is offsite data storage. Most of our clients still physically transfer backup files to an offsite records retention center. Recently, the participants in my Control and Security of Wireless Networks class and I went on a drive to identify poorly secured networks. We found an offsite storage courier van, unattended, in a no parking zone. It was monitored for over twenty minutes, and could have been monitored even longer. We were tempted to call the police to have the van towed, as it was blocking a fire lane. Imagine the look on the driver's face when he returned with client tapes and found his truck missing!

Concern about the physical transfer of files is not unfounded. I know of two clients who had their offsite files picked up by phony couriers minutes before the real couriers arrived. In spite of formal transfer procedures, these crooks were able to gain access to the files and the data contained within them. As a result of these events, I now recommend remote archiving via the network over the physical transfer of files by courier. Yes, this requires a high-speed network connection to your alternate site or your remote archiving service provider, but it certainly reduces the risk. For added protection, the files should be encrypted during transfer.

The risks described in this section are serious and there is a strong need to put controls in place to ensure that they do not occur. Controls are essential to conducting business in an electronic environment. While many of our clients are implementing very complex and technical solutions to E-commerce risk (encryption, secure communication through the Internet, etc.), we cannot over-emphasize the need for traditional physical and logical security.

SPECIFIC THREATS TO E-COMMERCE

High on the list of specific threats to E-commerce is the possibility that your network might be penetrated. Your network is subject to Internet attacks by cyber terrorists, electronic espionage agents, or simply your local neighborhood hacker. Your network could also be compromised through a trading partner's net-work. Modem attacks are also high on my list of threats to E-commerce. While you may have a strong firewall to protect your E-commerce environment from Internet attacks, poorly secured modems present a serious threat because they bypass the firewall and may provide hackers with complete access to your inter-nal network.

Poor authentication procedures are next on the list of threats. Account names and passwords are still the primary authentication technique. I believe that password protected access is past its useful life, thanks to password crack-ers and fast processors. As much as I pontificate on this issue, I still find that auditors and security professionals are continually sentenced to never-ending meetings on how long a password should be and the composition of the pass-word. I have seen people argue for several days over whether a password should be five or six characters long. The composition of the password is also debated. Should passwords contain alphabetic characters, numeric characters, or special characters? After many meetings and much discussion, the conclusion is usu-ally that users are not smart enough to select and remember complex pass-words. The issue is then put back on the shelf for another two years, then it is debated again, ad nauseum.

The technique I like to use to end the debate is to simply load a password file into a password cracker and demonstrate how long it takes to crack. On a 3.2 GHz notebook computer, any eight-character, alphabetic-only password cracks in 32 minutes. Change the composition to alphanumeric (letters and numbers), and every password will crack in less than four hours. Add in the most common special characters and all passwords will crack in just under two days. Select an even more complex password that contains alphanumeric char-acters and some of the less common special characters, and all of the pass-words will crack in 17 days.

How good is a password policy that says you have to change your pass-word every 90 days (which is very common), if the most complex password can be cracked in 17 days? Obviously, it is time to end the debate on the composition, length, and retention period of passwords. Instead, let's start the process of encouraging the use of security tokens (such as SecurID), digital certificates, or biometrics (such as iris scanning or fingerprint recognition). Prices for these technologies are dropping.

Next in line after authentication techniques, unauthorized access by an authorized individual is a serious risk. As old as I am getting, I am still amazed at the number of people who have administrator access to servers. They all need it, or so they claim. On some of our audits, we have found over 10 administrator accounts on a single server without a password or with a password equal to the account name. We have only had two clients where we found that administrator accounts were properly restricted and had complex passwords.

The next risk is the cessation of normal operations due to Denial of Service (DoS) attacks. These can be external attacks on the E-commerce site or internal DoS attacks performed by disgruntled employees or contractors. Proper installation and configuration of firewalls, good fail over techniques, and strong computer incident response and resolutions procedures can greatly reduce the impact of a DoS attack.

Another serious risk is the risk of viruses, time bombs, and Trojan horses (more on these in a minute). It seems every couple of months a new virus is released and rapidly wreaks havoc on servers and workstations around the world. Whether it is the "nimda," the "I love you" virus, or a new one, those who do not keep their anti-virus software and virus signatures current will undoubtedly be affected by the more common viruses. Therefore, ensure that all servers and workstations are properly protected.

A Trojan horse program is another related issue. This is a program that is placed directly on your computer by a hacker, cyber terrorist, or disgruntled employee. It can perform many functions including opening a back door so the perpetrator can access your computer, data, and files anytime they want. It could also make random or intentional changes to files or databases. A popular Trojan horse is NetBus (port 12345 or port 20024). Once NetBus is placed on your machine, anyone who is familiar with the NetBus back door can scan for it using SuperScan (a free tool). If port 12345 or port 20024 is open, then the Trojan may be on the machine. The perpetrator then attempts to log in. If it works, the Trojan was present on the machine. If it does not work, then some other service, such as a printer service, is running using the NetBus port.

Software failure is also a major risk. I divide software failures into two types. The first is system software failure. Occasionally the operating system or related system software fails. This can be a one-time failure which is quickly fixed by rebooting the machine. It could be an intermittent problem. It may be caused by a certain feature or function in the application or a component of the system software creating a situation that causes the system software to fail. The last is a flaw in the operating system that can be exploited. Hackers are always looking for bugs in operating systems. When they find one, they figure out how to take advantage of the flaw, or exploit it (hence the name Exploit). The best way to prevent system software failures is to keep up on vendor patches. (A patch is a vendor-specified software change to correct a program flaw or security vulnerability.) Also, you should check with the CERT Coordination Center, a facility of the Carnegie Mellon University Software Engineering Institute (*www.cert.org*). Bugtraq is another good service to help keep up with issues that need to be corrected. You also should check the operating system or hardware vendor web site on a weekly basis to identify any new security issues and how to correct them.

The second type of software failure is application failure. This can be caused by poor program change control, as when an application or a program is modified and moved into production without proper testing. An unusual transaction or combination of transactions can also cause application failure. The general rule for avoiding these issues is to have strong program change management and rigorous testing before moving new releases into production. Also, try to restrict changes to authorized releases. Occasionally, someone will request a simple change such as the positioning of data on a particular screen or report. The change appears simple, however, the programmer may make an error or the change may cause the program to bypass a critical control. By gathering these changes up into a single release, they can be made all at once and properly tested.

Hardware failure can also cause E-commerce outages. Here the solution is hardware redundancy and a strong preventive maintenance program. I have one client in the Middle East that truly believes in preventing failure. They have multiple ISPs and firewalls as well as four fail over servers, two at a remote location. They are very well prepared to mitigate or completely avoid hardware outages.

One factor that can occur even with the best hardware configuration is poor vendor maintenance. While vendor technicians are normally well trained, they can make mistakes. When they do, they can cause prolonged outages. To reduce the risk of technician-induced failure, ensure that your trouble reporting system is used to track the quality of the vendor technicians. While most of our clients do track the time it takes for a technician to respond, they do not track the name of the technician, the length of time needed to make the repair, and the length of time between failures. Sometimes a poorly trained technician records that the problem has been corrected when it has not. This results in another service call.

Exhibit 3.3   Example of a Wiring Jungle
in a Network Room

Human error can also cause E-commerce outages. Simply tripping over a wire (see Exhibit 3.3) can cause an outage. Make sure that your facility is safe and the equipment is protected to avoid these unnecessary outages.

Network or ISP failure can also cause serious outages. In addition to normal redundancy for network and circuit equipment, you need to ensure that you are protected from carrier outages. This includes taking such measures as using several carriers and routing circuits through multiple central offices. (For additional information on protecting against network outages, see *Network Auditing: A Control Assessment Approach,* John Wiley & Sons, 1999.)

The last item that can cause a major outage is sabotage. Sometimes hackers, employees, or competitors may attempt to disrupt, alter, or destroy your E-commerce site. The best prevention is to ensure that your site is secure. E-commerce vulnerability testing should be performed on a regular basis (at least monthly for critical sites). In addition, vendor patches should be installed on a timely basis and your E-commerce site should be physically secure.

As you can see, they are many things that can affect the performance and survivability of your E-commerce site. Much can go wrong. It is imperative that strong controls be in place to ensure that your site is both physically and logically secure.

CRYPTOGRAPHY AND ENCRYPTION

As demonstrated earlier in this chapter, account names and passwords are not good enough to protect our data. Not only is data exposed by unauthorized access on the servers, but it is also exposed in transit between the client site and your E-commerce site. One of the best methods of protecting data is to encrypt it. I have been recommending encryption for over 20 years, but other than the simple use of secure socket layer (PORT 443) to safeguard communications between two sites, very little has been done. Fortunately, new laws, such as HIPAA (Health Insurance Portability and Accountability Act of 1996), Gramm Leach Bliley Act, and so forth, are forcing executives to seek better and safer means to protect their customers' and their own data while in transit on the network or while it is stored on a server. Stories of stolen identities and compromised ATM and credit cards are two examples of how E-commerce data can be abused if it is intercepted.

Encryption is not as simple as it appears. It requires a lot of forethought and planning to implement. Some simple yet important questions that need to be answered are:

- Shall we use public or private key encryption?
- How will we manage keys?
- What level of overhead do we want to accept?

These questions have to be answered before your organization can determine the desired encryption philosophy. Before we go any further, there are some terms that need to be defined (see Exhibit 3.4).

SYMMETRIC CRYPTOSYSTEMS

The symmetric cryptosystems methodology is tried and true, having been used since the early days of business computing. It is simple and effective as it uses a private key to both encrypt and decrypt the data. The Data Encryption Standard (DES), originally invented by IBM, was one of the best and most popular examples of a symmetric cryptosystem. Various computer vendors have incorporated

Exhibit 3.4 Encryption Terminology

Item	Meaning
Advanced Encryption Standard (AES)	This is the new encryption standard that the U.S. Department of Commerce is working on to replace DES.
Asymmetric cryptosystem	This uses two types of keys, one to encrypt plaintext and the other to decrypt data. The private key is kept secret and is sometimes called the secret key. The public key is shared with trading partners so that they can use it to decrypt messages you send to them and encrypt messages they send to you.
Authentication mode	The process that decrypts an asymmetric crypto (public key). It also forms the basis of the digital signature.
Block cipher	A block cipher encrypts and decrypts data in segments of fixed length blocks (DES is a block cipher).
Cryptosystem	This is a pair of related mathematical formulae that can be used to encrypt and decrypt data. It is commonly called encryption, yet is really the encryption and decryption algorithms.
Data Encryption Standard (DES)	This symmetric cryptosystem was created for the U.S. Department of Commerce by IBM. It was first used in the government for encrypting unclassified data. Financial institutions adopted it as an industry wide standard in 1981. It is no longer considered secure, as Michael Wiener proved it could be cracked in $3\frac{1}{2}$ hours with modern technology.
Decryption algorithm	The formula that is applied to ciphertext that converts it back into plaintext.
Decryption key	A value that is used by the decryption algorithm to decrypt data.
DES	See Data Encryption Standard.
Encryption algorithm	The formula that is applied to plaintext to covert it to ciphertext.
Encryption key	A value that is used by the encryption algorithm to encrypt data.

Exhibit 3.4   Encryption Terminology *(Continued)*

Item	Meaning
Encryption mode	The process of encrypting data.
Integrity check value	This is the result of a calculation on the data that is created before the message is transmitted. It is used to ensure that the message has not been altered during transmission. The receiver recomputes the integrity check value when the message is received and compares it to the original. A secret key is used to prevent unauthorized tampering with the message and the integrity check value.
Irreversible public key cryptosystem	This cryptosystem can only be used in authentication mode (decryption only).
Keyed hash function	This is similar to an integrity check value. It is computed using a mathematical function to create a meaningless value called a hash.
Plaintext	Unencrypted data.
Private key	The data value that is used in asymmetric cryptosystems. It is the nonpublic key that is used to encrypt and decrypt messages from parties that use the public key to encrypt the message.
Private key crypto	See symmetric cryptosystem.
Public key	The data value that is used in asymmetric cryptosystems. It is the key that is used to encrypt messages to a party that will use the private key to decrypt the message.
Public key crypto	See asymmetric cryptosystem.
Reversible public key cryptosystem	This is a public key cryptosystem that can both encrypt and decrypt.
RSA algorithm	This is a very popular public key cryptosystem. It is based on factoring very large numbers. The original cryptosystem, RSA-129, was beaten after 17 years. By increasing the size of the numbers, the algorithm still has a very long useful life. The 515-bit modulus is strong enough for current technology, but the useful life is dependent on the processing power of newer computers. The prevailing thought is to use a 1024-bit modulus, just to be safe.

(continues)

Exhibit 3.4   Encryption Terminology *(Continued)*

Item	Meaning
SKIPJACK	Commonly called the clipper chip, it was intended to enable cheap universal encryption that was chip based. The algorithm is not public and the law enforcement agencies have back doors to enable them to decrypt data. This encryption methodology was not accepted by the public because of the back doors.
Stream cipher	This technique encrypts and decrypts the entire data message to create a ciphertext. Sometimes stream cipher uses a series of block ciphers to process the message into a stream.
Symmetric cryptosystems	This uses a private key to encrypt and decrypt data. The key must be shared by the sending and received parties, presenting the issue of key distribution techniques.
Triple DES	This extends the life of the DES algorithm by encrypting the message multiple times using different 56-bit keys for each encryption. Not a bad approach, but it is murder on the CPU.
Untrusted environment	For electronic commerce, this is the combination of processors, storage devices, networks, and VANs that data must pass though to get to the trading partner. No public data should be transmitted as ciphertext.

it into their products. While it is old, it is still useful for transmitting data. As with most forms of encryption, an export license may be required before you can send it overseas to your subsidiaries. For years DES was an excellent standard, but now fast computers have negated many of its benefits. Since there are only 70,000,000,000,000,000 combinations, modern parallel supercomputers can crack it fairly quickly. As a result, it has been replaced in most financial institutions by Triple DES or other more complex algorithms.

Encryption itself is a simple process. To encrypt data, the plaintext is put through the encryption algorithm. The encryption key is used to encrypt the plaintext using the encryption algorithm one block at a time (block cipher method). The encrypted data, or ciphertext, is transmitted and decrypted by the receiving party using the same key. Integrity check values can be used to ensure the message has not been altered. This provides protection in case the encryption key is compromised. If someone knows the key and changes the message, the integrity check will detect it. Because the integrity check uses a different algorithm (secret key), altering a message could only occur if the insider knew both algorithms.

ASYMMETRIC CRYPTOSYSTEMS

The asymmetric cryptosystem uses both a public and a private key. The public key is distributed to trading partners while the private key is kept secret. There are many advantages to asymmetric cryptosystems such as:

- Key distribution is automated.
- The public key can be posted on the Internet so anyone sending you a message can use it.
- The receiver of the message is certain that the message came from the sender, because only the sender's private key can encrypt the message (provided the private key has not been compromised).

The caveat: There are also some disadvantages to asymmetric cryptosystems. The first is that the larger and longer the encryption key, the better the encryption. Currently it is recommended that 2048-bit encryption be used. This increases the encryption overhead somewhat; however, with newer, faster machines, this is not a significant issue.

KEY MANAGEMENT AND TRANSFER TECHNIQUES

Key management for cryptosystems is very complex indeed! Keys must be created in a secure manner and stored until they are needed. Access to the key in a symmetric cryptosystem will give the holder the ability to decrypt intercepted data or to encrypt false data and insert it into your data stream. Keys must also be exchanged in a secure manner, to ensure they are not compromised. This can be accomplished by using a trusted human courier (not very good), or by encrypted transmission using a master key, or by using a public private key (asymmetric) encrypted transmission.

Lost keys present a serious problem. Once a key is lost, the data may never be able to be read again. This is the perfect information hostage scenario. Steal the keys after data has been encrypted, delete the official keys, and then ransom the keys back to the data owner. If keys fall into the wrong hands, an unauthorized individual could use them to compromise otherwise protected data. Therefore, ensure the keys are stored securely, backed up in a safe place and, if possible, stored encrypted to reduce the likelihood that they could be compromised.

Key retention is also an issue. Keys must be retained at least as long as the data is retained. To facilitate this process, it is best that encrypted data be cataloged by retention date. Premature destruction could be disastrous both in terms of cost and the business impact. Key backup is required to ensure that lost or prematurely destroyed keys can be replaced, just in case someone errs and destroys a key before the data is decrypted. Exhibit 3.5 contains some important definitions related to key management.

Exhibit 3.5   Key Management Definitions and Descriptions

Item	Meaning
Cryptanalysis	The process of cracking a cryptosystem. The greater the amount of ciphertext and the longer a key is used, the greater the chances of cracking the message.
Cryptoperiod	The official lifetime for a specific key. Keys can be generated and stored until the effective date, then no longer used at the end of the cryptoperiod.
Key authority	This is the location where keys are stored and secured after they are registered (e.g., a safe in a locked and alarmed room in the office of the bank's chief cryptographer).
Key backup and recovery	Keys must be stored in a safe location in case the original key is lost or destroyed by a disgruntled cryptographer. The keys must be retained until all of the encrypted data is no longer required. In some cases, this means forever. In other cases it might be 3, 7, or 50 years.
Key destruction	This process completely destroys all copies of keys when they are no longer required. Different parties may have different retention requirements. A bank service center needs the key during the cryptoperiod; their keys must be completely eradicated when they are no longer required. However, some data having a longer retention period may be stored at the service center. If this data is retained for electronic evidence or for historical reasons, other secure copies of the keys will need to be retained until the data is no longer required. Keys also may be destroyed when the data is to be permanently sealed so that no one will ever be able to decrypt it.

Exhibit 3.5 Key Management Definitions and Descriptions *(Continued)*

Item	Meaning
Key distribution	This is the process of delivering the new keys to the correct processes by the required date and time. There also needs to be an emergency key distribution for use when events dictate that the keys must change immediately.
Key escrow	Copies of all keys are held by an independent, secure, trusted third party in case the backup is lost or destroyed. In some cases, the authorities may require the keys to decrypt data for a criminal investigation.
Key generation	This is the process of creating a key. It must, repeat *must,* be truly randomized to reduce the likelihood that a cryptanalyst can predict the key and use it to crack the cipher.
Key management center	A key management center is a central authority that creates keys for use by two entities. The center creates a key for one of the parties and delivers the key to the other party encrypted. The party then encrypts the key using the master key, and then transmits it to the second site. The second site receives the new key and uses it to decrypt the data.
Key registration	This is the process of binding a key to the actual process it will be used for, such as registering the key for a digital signature. Keys are normally registered with a key authority.
Key revocation	This process is used when facts indicate that a key may have been compromised. They may also be revoked when staff are transferred or terminated. The data is decrypted, then reencrypted using a new key.
Key-encrypting keys	These are used to encrypt session keys when they are being communicated between sites and/or systems.
Master keys	These are keys that are used to protect other keys when they are transmitted electronically or manually. Master keys are only transmitted manually by a very trusted individual.
Session keys	These are used to protect large volumes of data as it is being transferred. They are also known as primary keys.

DIGITAL SIGNATURES AND OTHER
AUTHENTICATION TECHNIQUES

Digital signatures help assure that the sender actually sent the message and that the message has not been altered. This fits the criteria for establishing nonrepudiation, a core concept in the legal aspects of electronic commerce. There are two major models in common usage (DSA and RSA). They both use the same basic concept to ensure the message was indeed from the sender and has not been altered. A hashing function is applied to the message to create a message digest. This message digest is encrypted and attached to the message. Then the message is transmitted to the recipient. The recipient then runs the plaintext of the message through the hashing function to create the expected digest. The signature is decrypted to create the actual digest. The actual digest and the expected digest are compared; if they are equal, then the message is authentic (unless the private key has been compromised). If they are not equal, then the message has been altered. Exhibit 3.6 provides more definitions to assist you with the terminology.

Exhibit 3.6   Digital Signature Terms and Descriptions

Item	Meaning
Digital signature	A method of verifying that the message was created by the sender and that is has not been altered since its creation.
Digital Signature Algorithm (DSA) scheme	This is the National Institute of Standards and Technology (NIST) standard that is used to create a digital signature. The resulting signature is made up to two 160-bit values. The DSA standard is not used to encrypt the data, just to create a digital signature.
Digital signature for nonrepudiation	A digital signature confirms that the message originated from the sender and enables the receiver to know not only that the sender sent the message, but also from a legal standpoint, the sender cannot refute the transaction.
Elliptic Curve Digital Signature Algorithm (ECDSA)	This is currently under development by the Institute of Electrical and Electronics Engineers (IEEE). It will use algorithms that have less overhead to compute and are ideal for smart cards, which have limited processing capabilities.

Exhibit 3.6 Digital Signature Terms and Descriptions *(Continued)*

Item	Meaning
Hash function	In relation to a digital signature, a hash function is applied to the message and used to create a message digest that is encrypted using the private key of the sender, attached to the message, and sent to the recipient. It is a one-way function. Both the sender and receiver have to compute the message digest from the plaintext message. This ensures that a new hash cannot be created for a message that has been altered.
Message digest	This is a fixed-length result of a hashing function that is encrypted using the sender's private key. When encrypted, it becomes the digital signature of the sender. Because of the two-step process, the hashing and the encryption, the receiver knows with certainty that the sender created the message and that the message was not altered. This fulfills the nonrepudiation requirement for electronic commerce.
Sign	This is the process of performing a signing operation to create a digital signature.
Signature	The output of a calculation that is attached to the message to create a digital signature.
RSA Digital Signature Algorithm	This algorithm is similar to the DSA; however, it also enables the message to be encrypted as well as the digital signature.

The following risk/control table and checklist are what we use at Canaudit to identify the potential risks in a particular audit and the suggested solutions to mitigate those risks. The checklists are developed from the risk/control tables. They are provided to the client about 40 days before the audit so they can complete them prior to our arrival. The use of the checklists greatly reduces the amount of interview time required to gain an understanding of the controls in place.

RISK/CONTROL TABLE

Risk	Control	Status
A failure to protect the processing environment increases the likelihood of a prolonged outage.	Perform regular general controls audits at all major processing sites. Audit guides are available in several courses, such as Canaudit's, to assist in this effort.	
If logical security is breached on any server or on the mainframe, the entire network is threatened. A network penetration can result in the loss or destruction of program and data files. The network could also be penetrated from the Internet, a trading partner's network, or a demon dial attack.	Perform a full interconnected network audit encompassing both the network and the operating systems within the network. In addition, the network should be penetration tested by an experienced audit team.	
Viruses, time bombs, or Trojan horses could be inserted into the network, causing serious damage. Contractors or disgruntled employees could plant these in conjunction with their work, thereby creating or modifying programs.	Program change management must be in place. Also, independent testing of critical data should be performed by the quality control group.	
Information terrorists could attack the network, disrupting or destroying your electronic commerce application or taking critical files, such as the receivables file, hostage.	Ensure that the operating systems are hardened and that there is preemptive security function on guard on a 24/7 basis.	
Software failures could interrupt your electronic commerce operations.	Strong controls and testing procedures are required over vendor software changes. This	

Risk	Control	Status
Vendors could update the production version of your software with poorly tested code, causing an outage.	is difficult if there are no on-site programming and support staff to maintain the application. Measures should be taken to reduce reliance on the external software provider.	
The accidental destruction of data files could result in an inability to recover essential information.	Strong backup and recovery procedures are required, with frequent offsite backup.	
As dependence on electronic commerce grows, a minor outage can have a severe business impact.	Business continuance plans should be designed, implemented, and tested. The plan should include a series of "hot" servers at multiple locations, plus the provision to move to other facilities in the event of a full-blown disaster.	
A failure to use encryption can result in the unauthorized disclosure of customer or corporate information. This disclosure could lead to fraud or litigation.	All data transmitted or stored in the electronic commerce environment should be analyzed. Any sensitive or confidential data should be encrypted when stored and when transmitted.	
Use of the DES encryption standard can result in premature "cracking" of the encryption key.	Use the triple DES or RSA encryption or other more secure algorithms.	
The use of a public key cryptosystem for transmitting large volumes of data can create excessive processor overhead for both the encryption and decryption procedures.	Use a symmetric cryptosystem for transmitting large volumes of data.	

(continues)

Risk	Control	Status
If the algorithms are discovered, unauthorized changes could be made to the ciphertext. This may go undetected, as there is an unrealistic trust in the cryptosystem.	Use integrity check values or a hashing function using algorithms that are not known to those who have access to the cryptosystem algorithms.	
Without strong key management, keys may be lost or prematurely destroyed. As a result, unauthorized individuals may be able to view the data, or the organization may not be able to decrypt the data when required.	A formal cryptography function should be established and staffed. In addition, keys should be backed up in a secure location. In some cases, key escrow may be required.	
Poor key distribution techniques could result in keys being compromised or lost.	There should be formal procedures for distributing keys. Some can be encrypted and transmitted with the master key. Others will need to be hand delivered by a trusted individual.	
A failure to use one-time encryption for regular data transfer can result in the data being decrypted by unauthorized individuals because the longer a key is used, the more data is available to assist the cryptanalyst in cracking the code.	A key management center should be set up to generate one-time keys for trading partners in the electronic commerce community. Kerberos or some other technique can be used to distribute the keys in a secure manner. (Kerberos is a mechanism to select and distribute encryption keys so that data can be encrypted and transmitted.)	
A trading partner may be able to repudiate a transaction by claiming it was altered after transmission or that it was never sent. This can result	Digital signatures should be used to ensure that data integrity has been maintained and that the message was truly sent by the trading partner.	

Risk	Control	Status
in serious legal issues and may affect the long-term trading partner relationship.		
Password crackers, which are freely available on the Internet, have negated the password as a viable control. Passwords can be cracked if a hacker can harvest the file containing the password or monitor network traffic using a network monitor or "Sniffer."	Alternate forms of authentication should be used. This includes iris scanning, SecurID cards, or challenge response techniques. In addition, passwords should be encrypted when transmitted through the network.	
A hacker who masquerades as a host can trap passwords.	For critical systems, two-way authentication should be used. The client should authenticate to the host and the host should authenticate to the client. If the host fails to authenticate, then the security group should be notified immediately.	
A failure to use workstation restrictions increases the risk of a successful penetration, as the hacker can penetrate from any address.	Users should be restricted to a series of workstations to enhance the effectiveness of the password control. Notebook computer addresses can be added to the workstation list to ensure that the users will be able to authenticate when they are traveling.	

AUDIT CHECKLIST

No.	Question	Yes	No	WP XREF	REP XREF
1.	**Is a general-control review performed on all mainframes and servers in the electronic commerce environment?**				
	a. Is this audit performed annually?				
	b. Does the audit include testing of logical security and operating system controls?				
2.	**Is the network audited on an annual basis?**				
	a. Is quarterly penetration testing performed to identify external weaknesses?				
	b. Is formal network monitoring performed as part of the security function?				
	c. Are operating systems in the interconnected network hardened to protect the data if the network is penetrated?				
3.	**Is strong program change management in place throughout the E-commerce environment?**				
	a. Are controls over contractors strong enough to prevent the insertion of time bombs, Trojan horses, or viruses?				
	b. Are controls over vendors sufficient to prevent unauthorized changes?				
	c. Are controls over employees strong enough to prevent a disgruntled employee from making unauthorized changes?				
4.	**Is the network protected from information terrorists or electronic espionage agents?**				
	a. Is there a 24/7 security function?				
	b. Is staff trained to identify signs of a penetration and notify the security function when they observe unusual activity?				

No.	Question	Yes	No	WP XREF	REP XREF
5.	Are there strong backup and recovery procedures for all servers in the electronic commerce environment?				
	a. Are all data and program files backed up offsite frequently?				
6.	Is there a strong business continuance and disaster preparedness plan?				
	a. Are hot servers or mirrored servers available to take over the moment a failure occurs?				
7.	Is encryption used to secure data as it is being transmitted?				
8.	Is sensitive data stored encrypted?				
9.	Is symmetric encryption used for large-volume data transfers?				
	a. Is there a strong key management function?				
	b. Are keys changed frequently?				
	c. Are one-time encryption keys used?				
	d. Is a key management center used to generate one-time keys in a secure manner?				
10.	Are keys distributed in a secure manner?				
	a. Are master keys used to enable automatic transmission of new keys?				
	b. Does a trusted human distribute master keys?				
	c. Are there strong procedures over master key distribution?				
11.	Is there centralized key authority to store keys?				
	a. Are new keys registered with the authority?				

(continues)

No.	Question	Yes	No	WP XREF	REP XREF
12.	**Are keys generated in a secure manner?**				
	a. Is the key generation algorithm truly random?				
13.	**Is there a key backup and recovery function?**				
	a. Is the backup location under tight security?				
	b. Are those with access to the primary keys prevented from knowing the location of the backup keys?				
	c. Are the backup keys inspected periodically to ensure they are accurate?				
14.	**Is there a key escrow function?**				
	a. Are the escrow procedures audited regularly?				
	b. Are the procedures for obtaining escrowed keys documented?				
	c. Are those with ability to retrieve the keys from escrow trusted?				
	d. Are there only a few such individuals?				
15.	**Are keys only used for a short period of time?**				
	a. Are there procedures to destroy keys when they are no longer required?				
16.	**Are there procedures to revoke keys when:**				
	a. Keys may have been compromised?				
	b. Staff leave or are terminated?				
17.	**Are digital signatures used to ensure that the sender originated the message?**				
	a. To ensure that the transaction has not been altered?				

No.	Question	Yes	No	WP XREF	REP XREF
	b. To ensure that the transaction cannot be repudiated?				
18.	Are password crackers regularly used to identify users with weak passwords?				
19.	Is two-way authentication used to ensure that both the client and the host are authenticated?				
20.	Are stronger forms of authentication used, including:				
	a. Challenge response?				
	b. SecurID tokens or cards?				
	c. Iris scanning?				
	d. Fingerprint analysis?				
21.	Are users required to sign on from specific workstations or addresses?				
	a. At predetermined time of day and day of week?				

CHAPTER 4

Certificates and Nonrepudiation

This chapter deals with one of the most difficult concepts in electronic commerce—certificates and certificate authorities. In addition, it covers an easier concept—nonrepudiation. A certificate authority issues digital certificates so that E-commerce trading partners can be positively identified when performing electronic transactions. You may wonder why this is necessary since most humans use a password to identify themselves to systems and networks. To be frank, the password technique is over 40 years old and has served its useful life. It is just too easy to compromise or crack passwords. (If you would like to download some password crackers, they are available at *www.canaudit.com/downloads.*) Therefore, stronger authentication is necessary for E-commerce transactions. Digital certificates are a very useful technique for ensuring that the transaction is authenticated.

Nonrepudiation establishes that neither party can, legally, back out of the transaction at a later date. There may be many reasons for each party to back out of a transaction. The buyer may receive a better price from another vendor. The seller may find that they cannot deliver the product at the agreed price or within the required delivery time frame.

For both digital certificates and nonrepudiation, we have to understand the technical and legal issues that must be resolved. E-commerce cannot succeed without the use of technology to conduct business transactions that are legally binding and cannot be disputed or withdrawn. This chapter will provide you with the insight to understand the need for both.

CERTIFICATES

Digital certificates are electronic identifiers that can be used to validate the parties to a transaction. The certificate itself contains the information to identify the trading partner and the entity that issued the certificate. Exhibit 4.1 defines the elements contained in a certificate.

Some of the elements of a certificate are easy to understand. The version number and certificate serial number are self-explanatory. The signature algorithm identifier needs a little more explanation. The certificate authority is the entity that issues certificates to an organization or a person. The parties to a transaction need assurance that the digital certificates of all other parties to the transaction are valid and current. They rely upon the certificate authority's digital signature to prove that the certificate is real and has not expired or been revoked. Several algorithms can be used to compute the digital signature. The signature algorithm identifier specifies which algorithm is used and the name of the issuer contained in the issuer field. Certificates can be used for a specific period of time, just as a credit card has an expiration date. Digital certificates have both a start date and an end date for the certificate, which I refer to as a "shelf life." Credit card companies send new cards periodically to current and desirable customers. Similarly, if the certificate holder's credit or transaction history degrades, the certificate authority is only responsible for transactions up to the end date (unless the certificate is canceled earlier).

The certificate holder is called the subject. Other parties may want to encrypt transactions for security purposes. To facilitate this, the subject's public key information is contained within the certificate. This element has two components. The first is the algorithm identifier that specifies the algorithm to be used. The second component is the public key value, which is the subject's public encryption key.

Sometimes the subject has a very common name. Imagine how many Gordon Smith's there are in the United States and around the world. In Simi Valley, California alone, there are two Gordon Smiths and we are unrelated. If someone wanted to do business with Gordon Smith, they would want to be able to distinguish between all of the Gordon Smiths who might have a certificate. The subject's unique identifier is used for this purpose.

The certificate issuer may also need to be specifically identified. In a large international bank, there may be 20 offices and each office may be able to issue certificates. Each of these offices would need to be uniquely identified. As you may have already guessed by now, the issuer-unique identifier provides this information.

The last component of a certificate is the certificate authority's digital signature. This ensures that the issuer is valid and that the certificate itself is legitimate.

As you can see from this brief description of the certificate, all of the information required to validate the subject and the issuer must be present and there must be a method to validate that the certificate itself is authentic. The next step is to ensure that the parties can rely upon the controls of the certificate

Exhibit 4.1 X.509, Version 3 Certificate Standard

Element	Definition
Version	This is used to identify the version of X.509. Currently there are three versions: 1, 2, and 3.
Certificate serial number	This is a unique number that identifies the certificate. The certificate issuing authority assigns it.
Signature algorithm identifier	This identifies the algorithm used by the certification authority to sign the certificate.
Issuer	This is the name of the issuing certification authority.
Validity date	This contains the start and end dates for this certificate.
Subject	The name of the entity that holds the private key.
Subject public key information	The subject's public key.
• Algorithm identifier	The algorithm used for the subject's public key.
• Public key value	The subject's public key.
Issuer unique identifier	This is an optional field used if the issuing certification authority has an ambiguous name. This can happen if the issuer name has been previously assigned to other entities.
Subject unique identifier	This again is optional and is used if the subject has an ambiguous name.
Extensions (n values)	This is unique to version 3 (and may be for forthcoming versions). There can be multiple occurrences of this field.
• Extension type	This is the type of extension (key and policy identifiers, subject and issuer attributes, certification path constraints).
• Critical, noncritical	This can be confusing, but critical only implies that a certain extension be present in the certificate. Noncritical identifies other items that may be present.
Certification authority's digital signature	The certification authority's public digital signature.

authority. Each certificate authority must meet stringent control requirements before they can be certified as a certificate authority. This is a rigorous process and some organizations do not qualify.

To get a digital certificate from a certificate authority, the person requesting the certificate (subscriber) must complete a certificate application to register with the certificate authority. The certificate authority validates the identity of the potential subscriber or they may rely on a local registration authority. The certificate authority authenticates the subscriber using two identification documents such as a driver's license, passport, and/or social security number. They may also want to run a credit check to establish a financial limitation on the subscriber. If the subscriber lives in Simi Valley, California, and the certificate authority is in Fort Wayne, Indiana, it is doubtful that the subscriber would want to travel to Fort Wayne just to show two pieces of picture identification.

The certificate authority may use a local registration authority to authenticate the user. This can be a bank or financial institution or other organization that provides the identification process as a service. A local registration authority may not be as well controlled as the certificate authority. Some certificate authorities use affiliated offices or branches in local communities to perform the function of the local registration authority.

Once the subscriber has been properly identified and the authority commits to issuing a certificate, they are normally issued with a life span. The start and end dates are embedded into the certificate itself. The certificate cannot be used before the start date and cannot be used after the end date. Certificates can expire or they can be revoked. One reason for revocation occurs when the authority has reason to believe that the certificate has been compromised. If the subscriber's trading pattern changes, or transaction amounts are unusual, the certificate can either be revoked or it can be suspended until the subscriber can be contacted to verify the transaction. Again, this process is very similar to that of a credit card. On several occasions, some of my credit card issuers have halted transactions that looked suspicious until they contacted me by phone or had the clerk verify my credentials. This normally happens when I do my Christmas shopping. Like many last-minute shoppers, I leave Christmas shopping until the end, then I go to a mall and, in 90 minutes, do 10 or 15 high-value transactions. To the credit card issuer, this fits the pattern of a stolen card, and for that reason the credit card company validates me before one or more of the sales transactions can be completed. The certificate authority can use the same types of controls to identify potentially compromised certificates and validate the subscriber before the transaction is completed. Excessive use, unusual transactions, and value limits (over the approved cumulative dollar amount attributed to the certificate) are just a few of the criteria that might be used to flag a certificate as suspicious. Exhibit 4.2 provides the terminology relating to digital certificates.

Exhibit 4.2 Terminology Related to Certificates

Item	Meaning
Certification path constraints	These are used to enable certification authorities to certify another authority. This enables linkages between certification authorities.
Public-key users	There are two types of public-key users. The first is the digital signature verifier. The other is the encrypting message originator.
Encrypting message originator	This is the entity that originates and encrypts message.
Certification authority	A registered authority that issues digital certificates to organizations and people after their credentials are checked.
Subscriber	The human or legal entity that is the customer of a certification authority.
Relying party	This is the entity that relies upon the certificate issued by the certification authority.
Validity period	This is the cryptoperiod for the digital certificate. Certificates expire as they too can be compromised. Therefore, certificates have start and end dates. Expired certificates should only be used to verify the signature on a stored document.
Certificate subject	This is the human or legal entity that processes the private key for a certificate.
Closed community	This is normally a private, rather than public group of certificate users. A closed community consists of a certification authority and the subscribers that are normally part of a single business entity.
Open community	An open community consists of a certification authority that is independent of the subscribers, yet may provide other services to the subscriber.
Subject authentication	Because it is possible that a subscriber's private key for a certificate could be compromised, the authority ensures that the subject is in fact the valid private key holder.
Private key protection	These are the controls that the subject, who has already been authenticated, places on the private certificate key to ensure that it is not compromised.
Certificate private key	This is the secret part of the private key/public key generation. The subscriber retains it in a secure manner.

(continues)

Exhibit 4.2   Terminology Related to Certificates *(Continued)*

Item	Meaning
Certificate public key	This is the public key that a certificate subscriber makes available to those who want to validate that the subscriber is in fact the subscriber.
Certificate key— pair update	Key pairs should be replaced periodically (usually based on the cryptoperiod) or when it is possible that the key pair has been compromised.
Subscriber registration	This is the process where a subscriber applies to a certification authority by completing a certificate application. The certification authority verifies the information based on meeting the entity in person and establishing the entity's credentials. A local registration authority can also be used to establish the credentials of the potential subscriber. This is a service that could be provided by a bank branch or insurance agency on behalf of the certification authority.
Local registration authority	This is an entity that verifies the identity of a potential certificate subscriber.
Certificate update	This is the process of generating new certificate key pairs for the subscriber.
Certificate distribution	New certificates must be distributed to the certificate subscriber and the community. The certificate can be sent encrypted under digital signature. Alternatively, it can be distributed using a directory service such as ITU (International Telecommunications Union) X.509, which is part of the X.500 standard.
Certificate revocation	This is the process of revoking a certificate. The certificate can be revoked upon expiration, or it can be revoked upon request by the subscriber.
Certificate revocation lists (CRL)	These are lists prepared by the certification authority to advise the public users that a certificate is no longer valid for current transactions. The CRL is a subset of the X.509 standard. Users can pull the CRL periodically to update their records. They can also pull them prior to accepting an E-commerce transaction. They can also be pushed or broadcast to the recipients. The broadcast method is used for more urgent revocations, such as for compromised private keys.
Compromised key list	This is a list of keys that may have been compromised. They are not to be trusted.

Exhibit 4.2   Terminology Related to Certificates *(Continued)*

Item	Meaning
Certificate suspension	A certificate can be suspended if events indicate that it may have been compromised (similar to credit card suspensions). They are noted on the CRL as "certificate hold."
Certificate of authorization	These certificates are issued to indicate that the entity or person is authorized to perform a transaction or the financial limits to which the entity or human is subject.

As you can see from Exhibit 4.2, there are many controls in the process. The relationships between the subscriber and the issuing authority fall into one of two types. The first is the closed community. This is a private community bound together by some common criteria. They could be the vendors that supply goods and services to a particular organization. For example, car manufacturers may have their own closed community. The certificate authority would be the manufacturing company and the subscribers would be the suppliers. Another example would be use in military communications. Command and control and communication structures can be automated if orders are confirmed with digital certificates. In this way, the field units know that the order is really from the commander and not forged by the enemy.

In an open community, the certificate authority is independent of the subscribers. It could be a bank, a government, a university, or a commercial company. In either of these communities it is essential that the subject be authenticated to reduce the likelihood that the certificate has been compromised. If it is believed that a certificate has been compromised, it is placed on a compromised key list. Other authorities check these lists regularly to identify suspicious certificates. If a certificate is revoked, it is placed on the certificate revocation list. These lists are updated frequently and are available to public users so they can check the certificate before completing the transaction.

NONREPUDIATION: REQUIREMENT FOR INTERNET BUSINESS

When one entity does business with another, they expect that agreements will be honored. Doing business depends on trust between business partners.

Face-to-face contact is a critical component in building a long-term commercial relationship. Also, "having a face to match the voice" is often mentioned when businesspeople meet for the first time. This is the reason most organizations that use E-commerce continue to employ sales staff to visit customers and seek out new ones. The personal touch is maintained through sales and marketing calls. Order transactions processed through the web are generally adjustments, outbound and inbound logistics (shipping), invoicing, and credit processing. This arrangement provides the best of both worlds: personal contact, automated transaction flow, and a high degree of trust between the business partners.

In a pure E-commerce environment, face-to-face meetings between trading partners may not be possible. Therefore, it may be more difficult to establish and sustain a business relationship. In most cases, organizations try a few transactions to test the products, service levels, delivery, quality, and problem resolution. Over time, they develop a level of trust or distrust with particular trading partners. Unfortunately, trust is not a reliable control. Many of us trusted Enron, WorldCom, and HealthSouth. Obviously, we need better controls in place to eliminate the reliance on blind trust.

Let's look at a business situation that justifies the need for controls as well as trust. Company X sells widgets that can be bought from many other vendors. When it is updating web pricing, it inadvertently lists $20 each for the price when everyone else is selling them for $50. (The 5 key is above the 2 key on most numeric keypads.) As a result, it is flooded with orders, tens of thousands of orders. At first there is jubilation at the number of new customers and the instantaneous order growth that is occurring. The company believes it has finally made its web portal a success. Then someone looks at the dollar value of the sales for the day and realizes that there will be a significant cash flow problem if it ships at the erroneous price. Well, what should it do about this? A major airline had a similar situation when the decimal point was shifted on the price of an airline ticket (e.g., instead of a price of $1,000.00, the ticket was purchased online at $100.00). The company said there was an error in its system and dishonored the tickets. While it took some heat in the press and had a few upset clients, it was soon forgotten. In our example, Company X could just dishonor the transactions and incur damage to its reputation. However, while that is a valid business decision for a major airline that can absorb the legal costs, for a smaller company, often this is not an option.

Another tactic would be to quietly change the price, then say that Company X never received the orders. Or it may say that its site was hacked and it will not honor the transactions. While this might foster some temporary ill will, many of their clients will get over it, or at least that is the thought. Rather than risking the reputation of a business, I believe it is better to build in the controls, in the contract and through other means.

Nonrepudiation of origin is a control that ensures that the message came from the sender, who cannot then rescind the buyer's acceptance of the offer. This is normally achieved by sending the message through a third party such as a value added network or a service provider. It authenticates the sender, saves a copy of the transaction, and then forwards it to the intended recipient. If there is a dispute, the evidence is transferred to the trading partner that requires proof that the transaction occurred and verification of the price or other terms included in the transaction. When using a third party, a service request is often used to obtain a copy of the original archived transaction from the third party service. Should there be a discrepancy, either party to the transaction can request it.

Another way to generate evidence of a transaction is to use a technique called mirroring or echo back, described in Chapter 2. This is used by many organizations and is a very effective control. When a transaction occurs, the confirmation is sent from the receiving party to the sending party. Most of us are familiar with the concept, as we receive an e-mailed confirmation of the transaction when we book an airline ticket or hotel reservation online. It serves two purposes. First, it confirms the transaction for you and second, it ensures that the e-mail address of the customer is correct.

For further control, the original message between parties should contain a digital signature and a time stamp. This will enable the requesting party to verify that the message was not changed in any way by the third party or during original transmission to the third party. Exhibit 4.3 defines items relating to nonrepudiation. This is followed by the risk control table and the chapter-end checklist.

Exhibit 4.3   Achieving Nonrepudiation

Item	Meaning
Evidence generation	This is used to create evidence that the transaction occurred. This can be done by an echo-back technique, or provided by a third party service such as a VAN.
Evidence retention	The evidence must be retained by the requestor of the nonrepudiation service, an escrow service to a third party that is agreeable to both trading partners (such as a VAN).
Evidence transfer	This is the process of transferring the evidence to the party that requires it (sender, receiver, and third party).

(continues)

Exhibit 4.3 Achieving Nonrepudiation *(Continued)*

Item	Meaning
Evidence verification	This is the process of verifying the evidence that was generated by the requestor and transferred to the requesting party. This could be the decryption of a digest, digital signature, and a time stamp.
In-line trusted third party	This is a technique used in nonrepudiation. The sender forwards the message to a trusted third party, who digitally signs the message and forwards it to the intended recipient. This method is an alternative to nonrepudiation by token. It ensures that the original message and the verification are combined and transferred to the recipient as one message.
Nonrepudiation by token	A trusted third-party token is an alternative to a third-party verification of the digest. In this case, the message is digitally prepared using a MAC code (Macro Authentication Code is a method of encrypting data by passing it through an authentication algorithm) or integrity check value, then transmitted to a trusted third party. The third party verifies the MAC or integrity check value and issues and transmits a token to the intended receiver of the message.
Nonrepudiation of delivery	This can be achieved by an acknowledgment with a digital signature, a token, or delivery by a trusted delivery agent. This is required to ensure that the receiving party cannot deny that they received the message.
Nonrepudiation of origin	This is required to ensure that the sending party cannot repudiate the message. This can be accomplished by having a third party validate the message in some way.
Nonrepudiation of submission	This is required to ensure that the sender of a time-sensitive document (i.e., response to a request for proposal) sent the message by the required time and date.
Service request	A service request for nonrepudiation must be initiated by one of the parties to the transaction. This can be specified in the trading partner agreement, or electronically (preferably through a third-party service to ensure it is validated).
Verification of digest	In a nonrepudiation situation, a third party receives the message from the originator and verifies the digital signature and digest. The third party also verifies the originator and may time stamp it as well.

RISK/CONTROL TABLE

Risk	Control	Status
Without a method to authenticate customers and trading partners in an electronic environment, a binding contract does not exist.	The trading partners should implement some form of electronic authentication such as digital certificates or Secure Electronic Transactions (SET).	
If certificates are not issued by a responsible, independent third party, no reliance can be placed on the certificate.	Certificates should be issued by a certification authority, upon verification of the subscriber's credentials.	
Certificates are based on public/private key crypto. (A crypto is an algorithm used to encrypt data.) This code can eventually be cracked. A failure to change the keys on a regular basis can result in compromised transactions.	Certificates should have a limited lifetime or cryptoperiod. The certificates should be revoked when they expire or when they may have been compromised.	
A failure to check the Certificate Revocation List (CRL) may result in the acceptance of a forged or invalid certificate. This could result in transaction repudiation by the other party, which could have a negative financial impact.	The CRL should be checked regularly to ensure that only valid certificates are accepted.	
If the authenticity of the certificate is not checked, it is possible that an invalid or forged certificate may be used. Also, an expired certificate may be used if the validity date is not examined.	The issuer and subject's unique identifiers should be verified to ensure that they have not been forged or altered. In addition to the certificate validity, the date should be checked to ensure that the certificate is in force. The certification authority's digital signature should also be verified.	

(continues)

Risk	Control	Status
A failure to monitor unusual transactions could result in the use of a compromised certificate.	Transactions should be monitored. When an unusual transaction is detected, the transaction should be manually verified and evidence should be documented. If it is possible that the certificate has been compromised, the certificate should be suspended until investigated. Once the investigation is completed, the certificate should be reinstated or revoked.	
A certification authority's failure to create a linkage to other certification authorities limits the usefulness of the certificate and the certification by the authority.	The certification authority should establish path constraint relationships with other authorities so that they may rely upon each authority's certification.	
If your organization is a certification authority for non-related subscribers, then the organization may be exposed to excessive costs, should a fraudulent certificate be issued or a subscriber be improperly certified. A relying party may seek reimbursement from the certification authority for damages experienced as a result of the poor verification procedures.	The certification authority should carefully verify the credentials of the subscriber before issuing a certificate. Also, if the risk of improper certification can result in excessive costs, insurance should be acquired to cover the risk.	
If the certification authority supports an open community, then the impact of improper certification is higher than if the supported community is a closed community.	Insurance should definitely be acquired if the community is an open community.	

Risk	Control	Status
If the certification authority cannot properly authenticate the credentials of a potential subscriber, then the subscriber may use certificates for invalid transactions or may not adhere to the transaction terms.	A local registration authority should be used when the certification authority cannot easily verify the subscriber's identity and credentials. The local registration authority should have liability insurance. The certification authority should have the right to audit the controls of the local registration authority or access to a third party review.	
A failure to secure private keys by a subscriber could result in the certificate being compromised. A failure to secure the private key for the authority's digital signature could result in multiple occurrences of fraudulent certificates.	Private keys should be properly secured to ensure that they are not compromised.	
A failure to transmit new certificate private keys to the certificate subscriber in a timely and secure manner could result in the subscriber losing the ability to conduct E-commerce transactions.	Private keys should be distributed to the subscriber in a secure manner, using strong encryption procedures. They should be transmitted before the existing certificate expires to ensure that the subscriber's ability to conduct electronic commerce is not interrupted.	
A failure to distribute the public key for a new certificate on a timely basis could prevent the subscriber from performing E- commerce transactions.	The new public keys should be posted in an X.509 directory service. Alternatively, they can be transmitted to the subscriber for forwarding to their trading partners.	
A failure to determine that the trading partner identified in a certificate is authorized to perform the transaction could	Certificates of authorization should be used to ensure the party has the authority to perform the transaction.	

(continues)

Risk	Control	Status
result in an invalid transaction. For instance, the entity may not be authorized to commit the funds or have signing authority for the transaction.		
A failure to consult compromised key lists in communities that use them could result in the use of a compromised certificate.	The compromised key list should be checked frequently to reduce the likelihood of accepting a key that has been compromised.	
A failure to achieve nonrepudiation can result in excessive cost by either or both parties to a transaction. If the originator of a transaction is able to repudiate the transaction, then the receiving party may suffer loss. If the delivery of the message is successfully repudiated, then the originating party may suffer loss.	Nonrepudiation mechanisms must be put in place to reduce the costs of dispute resolution and to ensure that E-commerce transactions continue to support the business. If techniques such as mirroring and echo back are not used, then more sophisticated techniques must be implemented.	
If nonrepudiation techniques are not in use, then a transaction may be repudiated when it is to the advantage of one of the trading partners.	A service request for nonrepudiation should be made for important transactions. Evidence generation, transfer, verification, and retention techniques should be used in response to a service request or as a normal part of electronic espionage prevention.	
A failure to retain copies of E-commerce transactions could result in the inability to prove a transaction or in repudiation.	A third-party service should be used in certain circumstances. Transactions can be sent to the service for verification of digest or the third party can be an in-line trusted third party.	

AUDIT AND SECURITY CHECKLIST

No.	Question	Yes	No	WP XREF	REP XREF
1.	**Is your organization using Digital Certificates?**				
	a. Do they conform to the X.509 standard?				
	b. Is the signature algorithm used and is it current?				
	c. Is the issuer properly specified?				
	d. Are the start and end dates valid and current?				
	e. Is there a procedure to renew certificates before they expire?				
	f. Is the subject name correct (very important when companies merge, as it is often forgotten)?				
	g. Are subject-unique identifiers used when required?				
	h. Is the certificate authority's public signature current and accurate?				
	i. Is the public encryption algorithm present?				
2.	**Are inbound certificates checked to ensure that they have not expired?**				
	a. Are all inbound transactions checked to ensure that the certificate start and end dates are within the transaction period?				
3.	**Are there procedures in place to ensure that inbound certificates have not been revoked?**				
	a. Is the certificate authority revocation list used to determine if the certificate is current?				
4.	**Are there procedures in place to detect potential certificate fraud?**				
	a. Unusual or out-of-pattern transactions?				
	b. Significant and sudden increase in volume?				

No.	Question	Yes	No	WP XREF	REP XREF
5.	**If your organization is a closed community, are the following items in place:**				
	a. Procedures to validate the credentials of new members?				
	b. Monitoring transactions of existing members for unusual activity?				
	c. Timely revocation of terminated members?				
	d. Suspension of member certificates if there is suspicious activity?				
6.	**Are there procedures in place to ensure that transactions are not repudiated?**				
7.	**Is a third-party service used to archive transactions in case of a dispute?**				
	a. Is there a process to request verification of a transaction or group of transactions?				
8.	**Is echo back used to confirm transactions?**				
	a. Is the trading partner notified to check the confirmations for accuracy and authenticity?				

CHAPTER 5

Protecting the
E-Commerce Environment

Now that you have a good understanding of the E-commerce concept, it is time to look at the design and security of your site. There are many horror stories in the press about web sites that have been compromised. The objective of this chapter is to assist you with the necessary controls to ensure that your organization does not become a statistic. Despite all of the news, most electronic business is conducted in a safe and sane manner. Given the large number of Internet transactions, those that result in actual fraud or disclosure of confidential information are small. The difference between being in the headlines and safe Internet business is the control structure that you build to protect your E-commerce environment.

PROTECTING THE INTERNET ZONE

Let's first divide the machines used in E-commerce into three zones, then we will look at the risks in each zone and the best way to protect against them. (See Exhibit 5.1 for a sample Internet connection.) The Internet zone is your connection to the Internet. Your web site will either connect directly to the Internet or go through an Internet Service Provider (ISP). The most important control in this zone is to have a properly installed and configured firewall. There should be a router between the firewall and the Internet to protect the firewall from direct attack. The services on the router should be carefully selected based on the functions you require. This includes port 80 (http, unsecured web browser connection), port 443 (https, secure http), port 25 (SMTP, Simple Mail Transfer Protocol) and secure File Transfer Protocol (FTP). Other ports and services may be needed, however each should be carefully scrutinized to ensure that the service is required. Some of our clients set up Simple Network Management Protocol (SNMP) so that they can use various tools to manage the devices. Unfortunately, SNMP can enable a hacker to gain the knowledge required to penetrate your site. This is also known as bleeding the information required to map your Internet presence. For safety's sake, ensure that this service is turned off on all Internet machines as well as all other machines in your E-commerce network.

The next essential control is a reputable firewall behind the Internet facing router. There are many popular firewall software products including Nokia, Firewall-1, BorderManager, and SunScreen. Obviously, you will have to research the firewalls that are available when building your E-commerce site and select the one that best suits your needs. For the Internet facing firewall, I prefer that the firewall be installed on a very well secured UNIX server such as an AIX or Sun server. These servers should be hardened and up to the current vendor patch level.

The firewall software should be installed carefully to ensure that it conforms to the recommended vendor installation procedure. Make sure that the Read the Manual (RTM) control is used to identify the vendor preferred configuration and settings and to install the settings and configurations properly. Also, ensure that the root account can only log on to the console and that the firewall is located in a secure location within a restricted area. As with the router, only required ports or services should be activated on the firewall. This ensures that only authorized and secure services will be implemented. Make sure that Internet Control Message Protocol (ICMP), commonly called ping, is disabled, as there is no need to respond to a hacker attempting to map your network. Also, ensure that ICMP requests are not transmitted through the firewall. This would permit a hacker to send pings through the firewall to document the machines the firewall is supposed to protect.

Firewalls use a series of rules to define who and what has access to and from your network. You can restrict inbound access using the deny function. You can permit access using a permit function. The same holds true for internal users on your network who want to go through the firewall to access the Internet. You can restrict users or restrict the sites they go to. Firewall rules are very complicated and must be selected carefully. Once they are defined, reviewed, tested, and approved, they can be put into production. Then they will have to be carefully monitored to ensure that they are not accidentally or intentionally changed. All changes to the firewall rules should also be reviewed, tested, approved, and then implemented. That said, there needs to be an emergency change procedure to modify the rules or install patches when a significant event occurs.

This puts me into a dangerous area for an auditor. Under normal circumstances, emergency changes should be tested before they go into production. Often, our clients have a procedure for emergency changes that permits changes to be made, then reviewed by management after the fact. With machines that connect to the Internet, new security patches need to be installed right away. The process for notifying customers of security issues and patches also lets the hackers around the world know of the flaw. The hackers then try to exploit the flaw before the patches are installed. The longer you wait before installing an announced security patch, the greater the likelihood that hackers will attempt to exploit your Internet-facing machines. Therefore, these high-risk patches must be installed first and analyzed later. There is a risk that the patch may cause an outage, so the machine image should be backed up before the patch is applied. If there is a problem with the patch, then the backup image can be restored. While this is somewhat risky, the risk of a hacker taking confidential information must be balanced against the risk of damage to the configuration. When the hacker risk is high, the patches must be installed immediately.

For a firewall to produce the required level of protection, the logging, intrusion detection, and response procedures must be effective and properly utilized. The intrusion detection function is looking for activity that is suspicious. This includes a ping scan (pinging machines within a specific range of addresses to identify those that respond), port scans, and software that attempts to connect to open ports. There are several tools that hackers can use to document your Internet and Extranet machines. One of the most effective is Solar-Winds IP Browser. This uses SNMP to identify machines and the ports that are open on them. Some careless administrators use a default community string (password) that SolarWinds can guess. Once the community string is guessed, system information such as the operating system and version, accounts on the system, the services that are open, and other information that assist the hacker in targeting your Internet site, is clearly visible. I have sanitized the results of a sample scan and have broken it up into pieces so that I can describe the issues. See Examples 5.1 through 5.4.

Example 5.1   Identifying Critical Machines

```
# Subnet_aaa.bbb.ccc.x fullscan.txt exported on 5/11/2003 2:51:27 PM
# IP Network Browser version 5.0.127

aaa.bbb.ccc.x5 : MARKETING ********* Here is the marketing server

aaa.bbb.ccc.x9 : FTP ******* Here is the FTP server

aaa.bbb.ccc.x0 :

aaa.bbb.ccc.x92 :
```

In Example 5.1, we documented the date and time of the scan as well as the version number. The first machine scanned had a name of MARKETING. This tells me that there is a good chance that this is a marketing machine. I did not get any additional information because SolarWinds did not guess the community string. Below this we have what appears to be an FTP server. We can expect that this will contain files that are uploaded and downloaded. The other two machines do not give me any information at all. At this point, I have identified two targets. Based on past experience, I would make the assumption that the marketing and FTP machines are Windows-based. We will discuss how to verify this later.

Example 5.2   Identifying a Windows Server and the Accounts on It

aaa.bbb.ccc.x6 : NETWORK OPS ***********Here is a Windows Server
  Windows NT Domain Controller
  Community String: public
    System MIB
      System Name: NETWORK OPS
      Description: Hardware: x86 Family 6 Model 8 Stepping 10 AT/AT
      COMPATIBLE - Software: Windows 2000 Version 5.0 (Build XXX
      Uniprocessor Free)
      Contact:
      Location:
      sysObjectID: x.x.x.x.x.x.x.x.x
      Last Boot: 5/10/2003 11:49:43 AM
      Router (will forward IP packets ?) : No

    Accounts
      *********** This lists accounts on the machine. Hackers can use this to
      check for simple accounts and passwords. See below:

    Administrator
    alex
    bob
    Guest
    martin
    sharon
    test
    TsInternetUser

  TCP/IP Networks
    127.0.0.1 255.0.0.0
      MS TCP Loopback interface
    192.168.1.1 255.255.255.0
    aaa.bbb.ccc.x8 255.255.255.0

Example 5.2   Identifying a Windows Server and the Accounts on It *(continued)*

UDP Services

********** The following services are open and subject to exploit

53 : domain
67 : bootps
68 : bootpc
135 : DCOM SCM
137 : netbios-ns
138 : netbios-dgm
161 : snmp
*************** Edited for brevity

Example 5.2 is obviously a Windows NT machine and is it ever bleeding information! Note that the community string has a value of public. As a result, SolarWinds connected to the machine and was able to identify that it is a Windows NT domain controller and that the system name is NETWORK OPS. The machine name tells me that it is probably used for network operations. If I were a hacker and could gain access to this machine, I would attempt to download the passwords. I expect that I will be able to crack the passwords that will let me access other machines on the network. But how will I connect to the machine? Well, one way would be to take the account names and try to guess passwords. However, because we can see that port 135 is open, I would first try NBTEnum or Cerberus Internet Scanner (CIS)—software tools that identify vulnerabilities on Windows NT and 2000 machines—to identify accounts that have a password equal to the account name or blank. If I find one, it is a simple matter to log on. If I log in with an administrator-empowered account, I may be able to download the encrypted password values and crack them. Since this machine is a network operations machine, I would do a search of files to see if any contain the value "passw." With luck, I will find a spreadsheet or Word document that contains valid account names and passwords that can be used on other machines.

By now you are probably wondering how to prevent this. The first control is to ensure that SNMP is not running on any machines that connect to or can be seen from the Internet. This will prevent SolarWinds and other similar tools from querying the machines. If, for some valid and justifiable reason, SNMP must be set up (and this is very unlikely), then ensure that the community string is not "public," "private," or any other easily guessed password. In addition to removing SNMP, I would also eliminate the Windows null session capability on the NT machine. This is done by editing the registry. Specific procedures are available from Microsoft. (If you are unable to locate them, please e-mail me.)

Example 5.3   Example of a Sun UNIX Machine and the Information
That Can Be Gleaned from It

Sun Microsystems SunOS
Community String: public
   System MIB
      System Name: XXXXXXX
      Description: XXXXXXX
      Contact: XXXXXXXX
      Location:XXXXXXX
      sysObjectID: x.x.x.x.x.x.x
      Last Boot: 5/12/2003 1:06:52 PM
      Router (will forward IP packets ?) : No
   TCP/IP Networks
      127.0.0.1 255.0.0.0
         lo0
      aaa.bbb.ccc.x9 255.255.255.240
         hme0
   UDP Services
      0 :
      7 : echo
      9 : discard
      13 : daytime
      19 : chargen
      37 : time
      42 : name
      53 : domain
      111 : sunrpc
      161 : snmp
      177 : xdmcp
      512 : exec
      514 : shell
      517 : talk

As you can see from Example 5.3, this is a Sun machine. We are able to
identify that the UDP services echo and chargen are open. These two ports,
when used in combination, can sometimes be manipulated to generate a denial
of service attack. By using chargen to generate characters and then echoing
them, the processor may become so busy that it cannot accept other processing
requests. Ports 512 (exec) and 514 (shell) are open. This means that this
machine may be susceptible to what I call the "R" command exploits. If there

is a .rhost file on the machine, and it is poorly configured, I may be able to get onto the machine without authentication as the .rhost file creates a trust relationship. This means that if a machine is defined in the .rhost file or a value of + is on a single line within the .rhost file, then users from that same system may be granted unauthenticated access. With luck, a hacker may be able obtain root access and "own" the box. Disable all of these services (chargen, echo, exec, and shell) on all E-commerce machines.

The domain port (port 53 above) can be used to download a list of your IP addresses and server names. This provides a hacker with a road map to your network. Depending on how descriptive the server names are, hackers may be able to identify your critical E-commerce assets. The root cause of all information gleaned from the machines is that port 161 was open and had a community string of public. Close port 161! If there is a strong and compelling reason not to close port 161, ensure that the community string is a complex password.

Example 5.4   Example of an Intel Router

aaa.bbb.ccc.142 : MARKETING NORTH AMERICA
   Intel Corporation
   Community String: private
      System MIB
         System Name: MARKETING NORTH AMERICA
         Description: (c) Intel Corporation, ER8210 Intel Express 8210 Router, Version 4.20

         Contact: XXXXXXXX
         Location: XXXXXXX
         sysObjectID: x.x.x.x.x.x.x.x.x.x.x
         Last Boot: 5/12/2003 7:09:31 AM
         Router (will forward IP packets ?) : Yes
      TCP/IP Networks
         xxx.xxx.xxx.1 255.255.255.0
            LAN
         xxx.xxx.xxx.2 255.255.255.252
            Frame Relay
         aaa.bbb.ccc.x3 255.255.255.240

      UDP Services
         67 : bootps
         68 : bootpc
         69 : tftp
         161 : snmp
         514 : shell

In Example 5.4 we have an Intel router. I was not familiar with this device, so I visited the Intel web site, consulted their support section, and downloaded the manuals. There are two problems with this machine beyond port 161 being open. One is that the community string is "private." As a result, a hacker may be able to download or change the configuration. The other issue is that the Trivial File Transfer Protocol (TFTP) is open. TFTP enables unauthenticated downloads and uploads of unprotected files.

As you can see, from the output of just one tool, a hacker would likely be able to penetrate this web site and do significant damage. Therefore, we need intrusion detection activated on the firewall to detect when a hacker is using an SNMP tool as in Examples 5.1 through 5.4 or through port scanners. Once a hacker is identified, the severity of the hacker's actions must be evaluated immediately. If someone is simply pinging a single machine to see if it is running, that is not by itself a serious event. If however, attempts are made to ping multiple machines, then this could be someone trying to document your Internet machines. The IP address of the offender should be blocked. If an SNMP scanner is detected, and someone is trying to guess the community string, that is a very serious event and the IP address should be blocked. The IP address of the offending party should be sent to its ISP and, depending on the nature of your business, you may want to notify the Department of Homeland Security, Information Analysis and Infrastructure Protection (IAIP) Directorate. This was formally NIPC (the FBI's National Infrastructure Protection Center). More serious attacks should also be blocked and reported.

Many of our clients take a more simplistic approach. If they detect a scan or other attack, they simply block the IP address and move along. As this course of action is often automatic, some non-security-minded firewall administrators feel that the firewall worked. Our concern is that automated blocking can lead to a false sense of security. When the Canaudit Penetration Team is testing a client and we are blocked, we simply use a series of dial-up accounts to log into ISPs in many different cities. As we are blocked, we move on and connect through another dial-up connection. While it may take us a week to document the Internet-facing machines in this manner, we still document them. The arrival of our audit report is often a company's first notification that their site was actually under attack and was in fact penetrated (fortunately by friendly auditors instead of nasty hackers).

You might ask why the firewall administrators did not notice. Well, they were relying on the firewall to block the bad guys and did not realize that determined hackers will proceed slowly and use various techniques to continue their efforts, even if they are repeatedly blocked. Some of our clients also have an expensive intrusion detection software package. We often find that these packages block anyone who attempts to connect to multiple ports within 15 minutes.

We usually use Nessus or nmap on these sites and, by slowing our software down to one connect every 16 minutes, we defeat the intrusion detecting software because we are not exceeding its scanning thresholds. The bad news is, it takes about two weeks to scan just one machine. However, a slow and methodical hacker may be able to defeat the control.

That leads us to the next important level of control. Firewall logs are required to document all activity. Even if there is intrusion detection software in place, the logs are still needed to document activity. While I cannot recommend a manual review of these logs due to their size (it is not unusual for a single day's activity to generate 500 megabytes of data), I do believe in automated log review. This usually means that you have to buy an additional software tool for your firewall to enable easy access and analysis of the logs. It is critical that the logs be analyzed to identify signs of hackers. This includes both the noisy instant-gratification hacker types who use deliberate and noisy tools and the slow patient types who try to stay under the radar. By triaging the events, they can be separated into three types. A low-level threat would simply be blocked and the offender's ISP would be notified of their activities. Medium-level and high-level attacks would generate a page to the security officer who could then determine if the attack merits special attention up to and including the involvement of the authorities.

A few more things should be mentioned about the firewall: Make sure that you disable remote administration on the firewall to prevent any changes except those that originate on the firewall local console. Then make sure that the firewall is in a very secure area, with access restricted to allow only the firewall administrators and a member of the management team. Also, ensure that all machines in the Internet zone are protected by the firewall. One unprotected machine will likely result in a successful attack which is not only embarrassing, but is expensive to investigate. Another thing that sometimes is forgotten by firewall administrators is to block all spoofed or private addresses. Only Internet addresses should be permitted through the Internet-facing firewall. Also, special care must be taken to ensure that all systems and servers are behind the firewall. Any machines that connect directly to the Internet will be unprotected and are likely to be attacked. Some users, particularly in a university or research environment, may set up their own unprotected Internet access. Even though you have a firewall located in the data center, the researcher in a remote lab is accessing the Internet directly and compromising your Internet security.

Another mistake that is often made by firewall administrators is to run services such as mail relay on the firewall server. While this saves the acquisition of a server, it can severely affect the performance and security of the firewall. Never run anything other than the firewall application on the firewall server. Lastly, I would like to repeat my recommendation that ports and services be restricted to those that are absolutely required and that the activity is forwarded only to the specific machine.

PROTECTING THE EXTRANET ZONE

Now that you have an understanding of the Internet zone, it is time to move to the Extranet side. There should be a router behind the firewall that connects the Extranet zone to the firewall. As with the router on the Internet side of the firewall, only required services and ports should be open. It is often necessary to have additional ports and services active on this router as your applications need to connect to the Internet-based customers. These services and ports are prespecified and provide a more secure method of connecting the Internet user to the Extranet-based servers and applications. That said, it is necessary to regularly scan the router to ensure that only the approved ports and services are active. If additional ports or services are active, then they must be investigated to ensure that they were not placed there by hackers. Before leaving the routers, I would like to add that some firewalls incorporate the routers into the firewall itself so that there is only one device. While the devices have been consolidated, there is no additional risk because the single unit performs the function of all three units.

Controlling VPNs

Many of our clients are now using a Virtual Private Network (VPN). A VPN enables customers, staff, and contractors to safely traverse the Internet through an encrypted data tunnel, or pipe, from their entry point to the VPN device inside your firewall. VPNs are now an essential service to connect employees to your network in order to submit orders, answer customer questions, and send and receive e-mail. Because encryption is used, these transmissions are far better secured than a simple dial-up connection to an ISP or a dial-up connection to an internal modem.

In order to use most VPNs, there must be two matching software products. The first is the VPN software on the VPN device itself. The second is a VPN client that must be installed on the user's workstation, whether the workstation is used by a customer or an employee. This client software handles the intricacies of establishing the connection and encrypting the data over the connection. The user still needs to log in and provide a password in order to access the VPN. However, one concern is that the VPN clients can generally be downloaded from the VPN vendor site and installed on a hacker's PC. This means that a hacker could download the required client, then attempt to guess a valid account name and password. To defeat this, I strongly urge you to use secondary authentication in addition to an account name and password. Secondary authentication includes a device such as a SecurID token or card, a digital certificate, or a biometric device such as an iris scanner or thumbprint recognition device. This ensures that those using the VPN will be properly validated before accessing your internal network.

Two other items must be covered before leaving VPNs and moving on to other topics. The first is a somewhat common but serious mistake made when configuring devices. On several occasions we found some Cisco devices that had port 80 open. Many security analysts and auditors are aware that there is a port 80 feature that can enable a hacker to download the configuration file of some Cisco devices. We have used this successfully on multiple clients over the last few months. The feature is simple to execute. First, run SolarWinds or another scanner to identify Cisco devices with port 80 open, then bring up your web browser and enter the following URL: *http://ENTER IP ADDRESS HERE/ level/16/exec/show/config*. Simply insert the IP address of the intended target where indicated. Hit enter and, if the feature is activated, a copy of the configuration will be downloaded to your browser.

Look for the passwords and the password types. If the device is poorly secured, the enable secret function (very strong password encryption, which takes longer to crack) will not be implemented and you can use a macro to decrypt the required passwords. If the device is better secured, the MD5 encryption will be in place. It may take several days or even a few weeks to crack the password, but since these passwords are rarely changed, the time to crack the password may not be a factor. Whether it takes an hour or a month, the result is the same; a hacker gains administrative access to the device.

Now onto the next step. Several of our clients were using Cisco devices as part of a VPN implementation. This is an excellent solution, provided you follow the instructions and advice of Cisco. For whatever reason, the administrators created other accounts on the devices that bypassed the VPN security (access tokens, certificates, etc.) so that the network administrators could log in directly from the Internet. We can only assume that they wanted this access in case the VPN or security mechanisms failed and they needed to get into the network from the Internet. Whatever the reason, when these accounts exist, and if the port 80 feature is active, it is a simple matter for a hacker to grab the accounts and passwords, crack them, and gain access to the internal network. See Example 5.5, which I have altered to protect confidential information.

Example 5.5   Example of a Poorly Secured Cisco Device

```
version 12.1
no service pad
service timestamps debug datetime msec localtime
service timestamps log datetime msec localtime
service password-encryption
service linenumber
!
hostname GORDS_HOST
!
boot system flash XXXXXX-9.E.bin
no logging console
aaa new-model
aaa authentication login default local
aaa authorization exec default local
enable secret 5 $1$FED1$lKGRGLhVgHXe/iK0
!
username letmein privilege 15 password 7 ****Encrypted value was here

username IMAHACKER privilege 15 password 7 ****Encrypted value was here
****************************Edited to end of config listing****************************
```

In Example 5.5 we were able to crack the passwords instantly, using a macro available from *www.canaudit.com/Downloads/downloads.htm.*

Notice that the account name and encrypted password are clearly visible. To make matters worse, in one case, the administrator's Cisco account and password was the same as his domain administrator's account and password. Once we had the Cisco device, we also owned the primary domain controller. We then breached the network and harvested all of the user passwords and cracked them. This not only gave us access to their servers within the network and the files on the servers, but it gave us send and receive access to their e-mail.

The second VPN issue is not using secondary authentication at all. One of our clients recently had a VPN where clients authenticated using the same accounts and passwords as they used on the internal network. We were able to penetrate the network using a modem connected to a poorly secured machine running PCAnywhere. This machine did not have an account or password requirement, there was no authentication, nor was the connection encrypted. This enabled us to download and crack the passwords needed to log into the VPN. While modems are nice, they are slow. With a VPN, we could navigate the network at broadband speeds. Using an account and password for a senior executive, we logged into his e-mail account and sent an e-mail from his account to the person responsible for issuing access security cards for a remote site. The e-mail asked the person to prepare access cards for myself and another person. All we had to do was go to the second location and we were provided with valid access cards that gave us complete access to their facility. The lesson to be learned here is that all VPN access should require secondary authentication using tokens, certificates, or biometrics. No exceptions!

Secondary Authentication

Since we already mentioned secondary authentication, let's cover the authentication server now. This is normally placed within the Extranet zone. In addition to authenticating VPN clients, it can also be used to authenticate customers who want to access their data. These customers may come in through the firewall on a secure http to view their account balances, make payments, or move funds. Some of our clients authenticate the customer credentials (usually a digital certificate) on the authentication server before granting access to the confidential data. A failure to authenticate customers in this manner could result in unauthorized access to customer information. At one of our clients, we were able to access most of their customer bank statements (at the click of a button) from the Internet because we found a spreadsheet that had the customer accounts and pins on it. At another client, we were able to view customer account and payment histories. Needless to say, as soon as we identified these control weaknesses, we reported them to management for immediate resolution.

Protecting Other Devices in the Extranet

The next machine I would like to discuss in the Extranet zone is the intrusion detection server. This may be a stand-alone machine or it may be incorporated as part of the firewall. In either case, intrusion detection is critical to protecting your Extranet. When your security is breached, the sooner unusual activity is identified and isolated, the better. When hackers break into your Extranet, they may have significant access. If the rules are set properly, then the security analysts or Extranet administrators will be paged so they can take immediate action. The difficulty is setting the rules properly. If they are set too loose, a hacker may go undetected. If they are set too tight, normal user activity may trigger alerts. Once the right balance is achieved, the set-up will need to be reviewed on a regular basis.

The mail server is also a target for hackers, primarily because it runs SMTP. Some versions of this product are poorly secured and subject to exploitation. As mentioned earlier in this chapter, the best control is to ensure that all vendor patches are installed and the mail server is properly hardened. I also suggest that anti-spam software, sometimes called spaminators, be installed on the mail server. Spam not only takes up bandwidth, but some of it may be pornographic, or insulting, or otherwise inappropriate for an office environment. In addition, some of the jokes that people forward can take up a lot of bandwidth. Personally, I believe that a joke now and then is not a bad thing, only excessive abuse is a problem. However, if lack of bandwidth is an issue, then e-mails containing large graphics files could be blocked at the firewall. Be careful, doing this could also result in blocking valid graphics, such as engineering drawings or advertising copy.

The web server is a very important machine as it is often the first server accessed by clients. Consequently, it tends to get a lot of traffic. Many of the Windows-based servers run a software product called Internet Information Services (IIS). This product has a history of security flaws and you will need to constantly check for patches from Microsoft to ensure that the product remains secure. Some of the code on the web server itself could also be compromised. This is particularly true of Common Gateway Interface (CGI) code. Ensure that this is properly protected and up to patch level because this and other poorly secured code could result in web site defacement. While altered code is usually easy to fix, the altered code can be very damaging to an organization's reputation and may drive some customers away from your web site. Therefore, it is very important to constantly review the security of your web content in addition to the web server itself.

Denial of Service attacks (DoS) could also be launched against your site. This could knock your site down for a short period of time until the firewall identifies the problem and blocks the attack. Distributed Denial of Service attacks (DDoS) are harder to block as they come from hundreds or even thousands of different IP addresses. When a DDoS attack occurs, it is a major effort to block the attack, often involving your ISP, firewall provider, and law enforcement agencies. Unfortunately, when an important Internet site is affected with a denial of service attack, the news tends to spread like wildfire throughout the Internet. It is prudent to have a press release prepared and ready to go stating that the site was under attack, the controls worked, and no permanent damage was done to the site. Security was never breached. If customer records were never at risk, then state that. Otherwise, do not mention customer records, as there is no need to fan the flames unless there is definite evidence that customer data was affected. This press release should be issued when your organization has a very serious DDoS that takes it offline for several hours. Better to announce it than to hide it and have someone else discover it and make it front page news.

Many of our clients have an FTP server. This is normally used to enable customers and vendors to upload and download files. Customers may want to upload requests for proposals or order specifications and delivery schedules. Vendors may want to submit proposals or send price changes or other related material. Hackers may want to use the site to house and distribute pornography, illegal copies of software, music, and movies. My first concern with an FTP server is that it is often called a sacrificial host by the web administrators. They consider it to be a convenience server and therefore there is no real need to secure it. This makes it a perfect target for hackers.

Let's start with FTP itself. File transfer protocol is used to send and receive files. The files are not automatically encrypted. If accounts and passwords are required to log into the system, the accounts and passwords are not encrypted either. The account information and the data are exposed as they travel through the Internet. Also, most FTP servers I have audited did not have intruder lock-out activated. As a result, hackers can run a tool called Brutus (available from *www.hoobie.net/brutus* or *www.canaudit.com/downloads*) to guess account and password combinations. If the hackers find a valid account and password, they can log onto the machine. If there is an unshadowed UNIX password file on this machine, they can take a copy of the password file and crack the password. They may also be able to use an exploit or series of exploits to gain root or administrator access. With this access, successful hackers can use the FTP server as a firebase to attack other machines in the Extranet and the internal network.

If a hacker can gain access to the FTP server, he or she may also be able to load a sniffer on the server. This may enable the hacker to trap data as well as accounts and passwords as they are transmitted through the Extranet or between machines on the Extranet. It is also possible to trick a web or firewall administrator into revealing his or her password. One trick that often works is to perform a short denial of service or distributed denial of service attack against the firewall. Once the attack is detected, the firewall alerts the administrator by e-mail or page. Most administrators then try to log into the firewall. If the attack is timed to be after hours, there is a good chance the administrator will attempt to log in from the Internet. When they do, the hacker may be able to sniff them using the FTP-server-based sniffer. This risk is very high indeed if the administrator is not using secondary authentication.

The next item to be covered is the application servers in the Extranet. These may be online customer ordering, banking, E-procurement, trading partner, or other types of machines. While there are many ways to build these servers and process client transactions, they boil down to one of two methodologies. The first is to use a technique that I call "dump the data over the fence." Many web applications permit clients to review their account data after the client is authenticated. To save traffic coming through the firewall, the account data for all online accounts is placed on the web application server one or more times a day. The clients can then view their data at the time of the last upload to the web server. If the client wants to perform a transaction, they can do so and it stays on the server. Periodically, the main application running on the server or mainframe within the Intranet collects the data from the Extranet application server. The benefit of this approach is that the customers do not need to come through the internal firewall to the Intranet. They can view their account as it stood at end of business on the previous day, or more frequently if the Extranet server is updated several times a day. They can also prepare transactions and those transactions can be edited. The application server on the Internet controls the pickup transactions and can then process them.

But there are drawbacks to this approach. The client may want current information. Also, the transactions are sitting in the Extranet. Should the Internet firewall be breached and if the web application server has a security weakness, then hackers may be able to get customer transaction or account information and balances. To avoid this, many web applications are designed to authenticate the client and prepare transaction requests. These requests are passed through the internal firewall to the Intranet application server. Only the requested information of the specified customer is retrieved. Transactions are validated much the same way. This has the advantage of providing the customers with real time data and ensuring that transactions are properly updated.

For further security, web transactions are encrypted before they are sent to the Intranet server for processing. The firewall should have a rule that permits traffic to go from the web application server through the firewall to the specific application server on the Intranet using a prespecified port or series of ports that are assigned to each Intranet application server. Now we have ensured that only authenticated clients can come through the firewall, the transactions are properly edited, the transactions are encrypted, and they can only go to the appropriate application server on the Intranet. We have also minimized the data that could be harvested by a hacker who penetrates the external Internet firewall and who gains access to the Extranet. Provided that all machines on the Extranet have been hardened and are up to current vendor patch level, then we have a well secured and functional E-commerce application.

PROTECTING THE INTRANET

It is now time to turn our attention to the routers and firewall that protect the Intranet (internal network). We have already described the configuration of the external Internet firewall. To refresh your memory, we used a hardened UNIX server (say a Sun machine) running a good firewall product such as SunScreen or Nokia. (Note: Remember to change the SunScreen default admin account password from admin to a more secure password. This information is available to anyone who accesses the Sun site at *http://docs.sun.com/db/doc/806-6345/ 6jf9uj72t?q=SunScreen&a=view*. Search for passw and it will display the default admin account with the password of admin. On the internal firewall, which is intended to protect the internal network should the external firewall and/or Extranet be breached, we have a different configuration. My concern is that if both of these firewalls are the same, running on the same operating system, then when a new exploit defeats the external firewall or the server that hosts the firewall, the internal firewall will be easily defeated. The solution is to use two different operating systems to host the firewall and two different firewall applications. Since I used UNIX and SunScreen on the Internet facing firewall, I would use a Novell server, hosting the BorderManager firewall product. If a hacker penetrated the Internet facing firewall, now he or she has to start all over to penetrate the internal network. If you are running an IDS, then you should be able to detect hackers before they penetrate the internal network. The internal firewall should also be protected by one router in front of the firewall and one behind it. This configuration will be used to block unnecessary services and block some penetration attempts.

BUSINESS CONTINUANCE: KEEPING THE WEB SITE ACCESSIBLE

Business continuance is also very important for your E-commerce site. In Exhibit 5.1, only primary machines were included. Points of failure that could result in a serious outage are:

- ISP or the ISP connection
- Internet-facing routers and firewall
- VPN and other critical servers in the Extranet
- Intranet-facing routers and firewall

As with all business continuance decisions, the effect of an outage—including lost business, damage to the firm's reputation, and dissatisfied customers—must be weighed against the costs of building in redundancy. Let's make the assumption that the Internet connection itself is critical. If it fails, inbound and outbound e-mail as well as customer, investor, and trading partner services would be completely shut down from an Internet standpoint. Because this could be expensive, it must be avoided, provided the costs of doing so are acceptable. If your web presence is just a catalog viewing site, then you could be down for several hours with no serious impact. If your organization relies heavily on E-commerce, then any failure would have an immediate impact on the business.

Exhibit 5.1   Sample Internet Connection

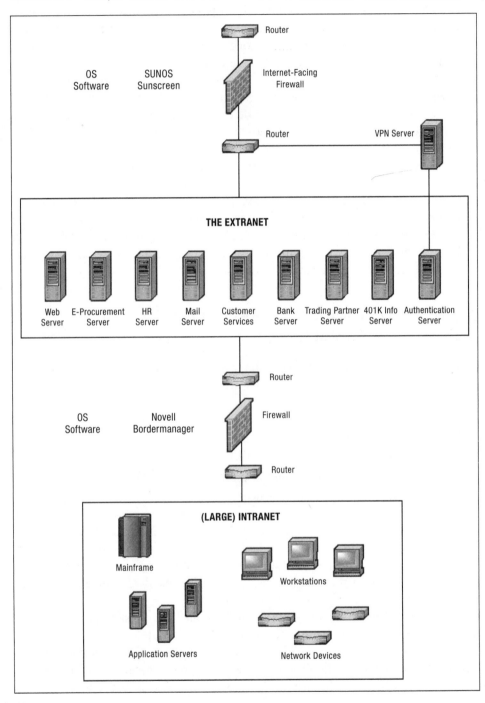

In most cases, connections to the Internet must be operational at all times. This means that we must build in the required redundancy. First, we must have a second ISP, one that uses completely different circuits. No point having two ISPs that connect to your organization over the same circuits. Keep in mind that one ISP may use AT&T and the other may use MCI, but just because they are using two different carriers does not mean they are using different circuits. Carriers often use each other's circuits. Also, while major carriers can certainly reroute your traffic around failing circuits, you have to worry about the link between your site and the carrier, which may not have the same redundancies as the full carrier network, particularly in smaller communities.

Once we have truly redundant ISPs, we have to worry about router and firewall failures. Firewall and router configurations should be duplicated as shown in Exhibit 5.2. By interconnecting the routers to the firewalls, if any router fails or either firewall fails, then the failing component can be bypassed while permitting transactions to flow properly and in a controlled manner into the Extranet. In case the Intranet-facing router and firewall configuration fails, this also should be replicated and cross-linked so that any failing device can be successfully and safely bypassed. Not only does redundancy greatly reduce the likelihood of an E-commerce failure, but it also can be used to provide load balancing. If there are sudden increases in volume or response time is slower during peak hours, then the replicated ISP connections and firewalls can share the load, balancing the transactions between the two ISPs and the firewalls.

Now that we have protected the ISP and Internet connections from a failure, the Extranet servers also need to be protected. Each server in the Extranet should be evaluated to determine if a failure or prolonged outage would seriously disrupt the business. Based on the information in Exhibit 5.1, I would replicate the web, VPN Authentication, E-procurement, customer service, and trading partner servers. If I had budget constraints, I might risk not duplicating the E-procurement and trading partner servers because I may be able to withstand an outage of, say, four hours or so. (If not, then these have to be replicated as well.) Accepting a reasonable level of risk is sometimes acceptable, as most problems can either be resolved in three or four hours, or another server can be pressed into service to replace the downed machine.

While the redundancy described in this chapter is meant for business continuance and load balancing, the design does not protect your organization in the event of a disaster. In case of catastrophic events, one option would be to place the primary and secondary Internet configurations in different locations. This would provide equipment redundancy, however it would require a high-speed network to connect back to the Intranet. Several Canaudit clients have a second site where they have preloaded servers and replicated data and programs ready to go online at a moment's notice. Another client has a full and complete replication

Exhibit 5.2 E-Commerce Redundancy

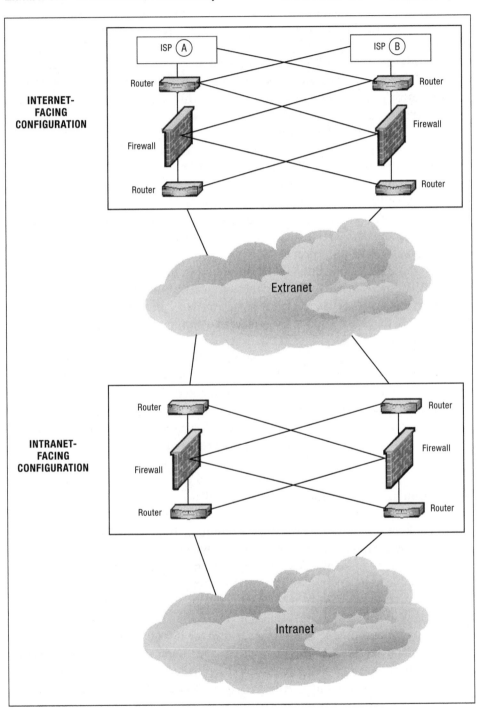

of the configuration in Exhibit 5.2 at a second site. This is not only ready to go but is fully functional and can stand in if the primary configurations are destroyed or subjected to a denial of service attack. Certainly this is the best approach if you have a large E-commerce business that is time critical.

Don't forget that your E-commerce business continuance and disaster preparedness plan must be integrated into the overall organizational plans. Also, the plans must be tested on a regular basis to verify that they function well and that if the E-commerce business server, connection, or network fails, the transactions fall over to the backup servers and circuits.

RISK/CONTROL SUMMARY

Business Issue	Suggested Action	Status
A failure to protect the E-commerce site could result in accidental or intentional disruption of E-business capabilities.	Ensure that the E-commerce site is properly protected with a series of firewalls and routers to protect the firewalls (called bastion routers).	
If the E-commerce site is not segmented into zones, when a hacker penetrates the external firewall, they will have complete access to the E-business site and potentially the internal network.	The E-business site should be divided into at least three zones. The first zone is the Internet zone consisting of an Internet-facing router that protects the Internet firewall from direct attack and an Extranet-facing router to protect the firewall from an attack originating in the Extranet. There should also be a firewall configuration between the Extranet and the Intranet. An Extranet-facing router is required to protect the firewall from an attack from the Internet or from within the Extranet itself. An Intranet-facing router should protect the firewall from an attack originating from within the Intranet.	

(continues)

Business Issue	Suggested Action	Status
If there are too many active ports or services on the routers, then the routers will not properly protect the firewall.	The Internet-facing router should have a limited number of services running. Permissible services are port 443 (secure socket layer, Secure HTTP, and Secure Shell). The mail service (simple mail transfer protocol) may be required if the E-business site also processes inbound and outbound mail. Also, unprotect http may be required to enable customers to view data on the web server. Other ports and services may be required; however, they should not be activated unless they are absolutely necessary and they are approved by both the chief security officer and management. The routers protecting the Intranet should also be limited to required services. Applications may require nonstandard ports to enable customer transactions to flow to the appropriate application server.	
If SNMP is active, hackers or other curious individuals may be able to view the machines used to conduct E-business. Also, if a default community string is used, the machines may divulge the information hackers need to successfully attack your E-commerce site.	Never permit the use of SNMP on E-commerce sites. Always set the community string to a complex combination of alphabetic and special characters, at least eight characters long. Setting a complex community string will reduce the damage that can be done should someone accidentally or intentionally activate SNMP.	

Business Issue	Suggested Action	Status
Ping (ICMP) can be used to identify the IP addresses and possibly the machine names of machines in the E-commerce site. If it is permitted to go through the firewall, the internal network may also be penetrated by hackers.	Turn off ICMP for all machines in the E-commerce zones. Also ensure that ICMP is blocked at the external firewall.	
The firewall software running on a firewall server can be attacked if the operating system is not properly hardened and secured.	Follow the operating system vendor's methodology to harden the server before installing the firewall.	
Firewall configurations and settings, if not properly installed and maintained, may result in the firewall being compromised. The E-commerce site may be compromised as a result.	Follow the firewall vendor's instructions for creating a secure configuration. Ensure that all settings are appropriate. Also ensure that the configuration is inspected and approved by a knowledgeable firewall consultant.	
If too many services are running on the firewall, then the firewall may be subject to attack.	Ensure that only required and safe services are configured.	
A firewall with too many rules or rules that have been poorly conceived will not properly protect the E-commerce site or the internal network.	Ensure that the rules are properly configured and that they do not conflict with other rules. Also ensure that the rules are reviewed regularly so that unauthorized or unintentional changes will be detected. The rule sets should be properly documented along with the justification for each rule.	

(continues)

Business Issue	Suggested Action	Status
Unauthorized changes may be made to the firewall, the routers, or the servers within the Extranet. These changes may weaken control and subject the E-commerce site to a successful attack.	There should be a formal change management procedure in place over all machines in the E-commerce site. This procedure should ensure that all changes are carefully scrutinized before approval. The changes should also be thoroughly tested to confirm that they work as intended and do not create vulnerabilities that could expose the machines within the E-commerce site to attack. Once changes are made, the E-commerce site should be subjected to a full penetration test to verify that it remains secure.	
When new vulnerabilities are discovered, hackers often immediately start scanning the Internet for susceptible machines. When they find one, they attempt to exploit the vulnerability before it can be patched. They may do significant damage to unpatched machines.	There should be an emergency patch procedure to allow all vendor security patches to be properly analyzed. Any critical patches should be installed immediately under the emergency change control process. The E-commerce site should then be scanned to ensure that no unauthorized services or new vulnerabilities exist. Before installing the patches, image copies of the machines should be taken in case the patch fails and the image needs to be restored.	
If activity is not properly logged it will be difficult, if not impossible, to identify an attack and the source of the attack.	Ensure that firewall logging is implemented and that logs are reviewed on a regular basis.	

Business Issue	Suggested Action	Status
Firewall logs can be quite large and difficult to review manually. As a result, significant events may go undetected.	Firewall activity should be classified into various threat levels. Automated alerts should be generated to page or e-mail the firewall administrators and security officers when a serious event occurs.	
If firewall events are not detected on a timely basis, hackers may be able to penetrate the E-commerce site.	Intrusion detection software should be installed and properly configured to ensure that all serious events are reported, yet legitimate traffic is permitted. This will require a very careful balancing act as sometimes normal activity appears similar to a low-level hacker attack.	
Occasionally a machine may not be protected by the firewall. As a result, it can be attacked and used as a firebase to attack other machines on your E-commerce site.	Make sure that all machines are protected by the firewall.	
Failure to prevent a user from gaining inappropriate access could result in serious penetration of the network and disclosure of confidential company, customer, or patient information	A multilevel response and escalation procedure for detected potential security breaches may be implemented as part of your emergency response. **Level 1** One instance of potentially unfriendly activity (finger, unauthorized telnet, port scan, etc.). Ensure the source is not an authorized employee using diagnostic tools. • Record user/IP address/ MAC address. • Warn user of their indiscretion and provide human resources with documentation of the incident.	

(continues)

Business Issue	Suggested Action	Status
	Level 2 One instance of a clear attempt to obtain unauthorized information or access (download password files, access restricted areas, unauthorized use of a hacking tool, etc.) or a second Level 1 attack. • Immediate human resources issue, which may lead to disciplinary action including and up to dismissal. • Research origin of connection. If the origination is from outside the internal network, refer to the *external* response. • Research potential risks related to intrusion method attempted. **Level 3** This is a crime under the Computer Fraud and Abuse Act (CFAA), 18 USC §1030. Determine the most effective counter-measure based on type and severity of incident. • Create evidence logs to provide to authorities so they can determine if criminal actions are warranted. • Install traps and sniffers for the evidence log. • Eliminate the intruder's means of access and any related vulnerabilities. • Research origin of connection.	

Business Issue	Suggested Action	Status
	Also, there should be a proper Computer Incident Response Procedure. RFC 2350 provides a guideline. It is available at *www.cis.ohiostate.edu/ cgi-bin/rfc/rfc2350.html.*	
Professional hackers may reduce the intensity of their attacks so that they remain below the radar of the intrusion diction software. As a result, these attacks may go undetected.	Periodically review the IDS settings to determine if they are appropriate. Also, be on the alert for very low intensity attacks.	
Professional hackers may detect when they are being blocked. If so, they may use other techniques such as dialing into one or more ISPs which gives them a new IP address every time. They may also use other evasive techniques such as launching their attacks from other penetrated machines or spoofing IP addresses.	While blocking attacks seems like a good control, to be truly effective, the blocked addresses must be analyzed. The question to be answered is whether the attack is a random event or part of a determined, yet well disguised attack against the E-commerce site. This may require the services of a professional forensics investigator.	
In setting firewall rules, some administrators block seemingly nefarious activities for a period of 15 minutes to one hour. While this is a strength, it can be turned into a weakness if hackers can determine the lockout period. Once they determine that, they can set their software to automatically resume the attack at a slower pace and lower intensity. When blocked, the attack will halt until the block time period has expired.	Create an alert for attacks that, while they may seem random and spread over a period of time, are all from the same hacker. Be aware that this indicates that a skilled hacker is attacking your site and you may need the assistance of the authorities or a professional forensic investigator.	

(continues)

Business Issue	Suggested Action	Status
Many Unix systems are running the "R" services, rlogin and rexec. These commands often allow a user logged into one system to log into another without supplying a password. These connections can be spoofed, allowing attackers easy access to the system.	Rexec, rshell, and rlogin should be turned off. However, if it is necessary to run these services for a specific application or other service, then these systems should be better secured. Suggested action: • Implement the use of ssh (secure shell). • Implement the use of tcp wrappers. This way the trust relationships will stay in place, but the sessions will be secure.	
The echo and chargen network services are often running on UNIX machines. These services enable a DoS attack to be run against the machines, which could have a significant impact on production.	Echo is sometimes used to test if a machine is up and running by sending packets to it and getting a response. If you are using echo, then chargen should be disabled; otherwise, both chargen and echo should be disabled.	
If the SMTP service is running on the Unix system and the "verify" and "expand" commands are permitted, then these commands will enable hackers to identify the accounts that are on a machine without authenticating to the server. This gives hackers a better chance of cracking a valid account name and password and decreases the time to penetrate a system. This is due to an excessive number of systems running the smtp service.	The "verify" and "expand" commands should be disabled on all SMTP running systems unless there is a proven need for this command to be activated.	

Business Issue	Suggested Action	Status
Rhosts and hosts.equiv files create trust relationships which can start a security domino effect. Once one machine is compromised, other machines trusted by the first machine will also be compromised. Sensitive files such as /.rhosts and /etc/hosts.equiv, which are responsible for setting the security on the rexec services, should not be set to world writeable. This allows any user on the system to add himself or herself to the trusted computing base and log in as any user from any machine without supplying a password.	Trust relationships seriously jeopardize security. The data in the /etc/.rhost should be removed and the permissions set to no read, no write, no execute for the owner, the group and the world. This blank, protected .rhost file will prevent hackers from placing their own .rhost file in the /etc directory. Other .rhosts files should be removed from the system. The hosts.equiv file also creates trust relationships and should be emptied and protected in the same manner as the /etc/.rhosts file described above.	
The password files on some UNIX systems are not shadowed; this enables anyone on the system to retrieve the encrypted passwords and crack them.	Insist that users follow the password policy. Passwords should not be dictionary words and users should change their passwords on a regular basis (every 30 days). Pluggable Authentication Modules (PAM) should be used to force users setting or changing their passwords to select a strong password. Also, a utility such as npassword, which is available on the Internet, could be used to enforce password complexity.	
Permissions on system cron table files are world readable. Cron is used to automatically execute commands on a	Permissions on all cron table files should be defined as being owned only by the actual owner of the table and	

(continues)

Business Issue	Suggested Action	Status
routine basis. These files should always be readable only by the owner of the cron table. By reading the system cron table, we were able to identify several shell scripts that were executed by root. These scripts were world writeable, allowing anyone on the system to execute any series of commands as the root user when the program executes. An attacker could use this to create a root-enabled account on the system and then execute any commands as root at any time.	permissions should be set to read only for that user, with no permissions for any groups and no world permissions. The following two commands will set the correct permissions for all crontabs if run as root (syntax is very important, no back-ticks): # cd /var/spool/cron/crontabs # perl –e 'foreach (@ARGV) { system("chown $_ $_; chgrp $_ $_; chmod 400 $_"); }' *	
If a firewall is running services and processes other than the firewall itself, then the effectiveness of the firewall may be compromised.	Ensure that the firewall is not running any other services such as mail relay.	
If users and administrators are permitted to log into the network from the Internet, their logon account and password may not be encrypted. Also, the data being transmitted may not be encrypted.	Use a VPN with a client software product to ensure that the sessions are encrypted.	
Many VPN users log into the VPN with an account and password and no secondary authentication. As a result, it may be possible for a hacker to compromise an account/ password combination and log in as a valid user.	Use secondary authentication such as a token, biometrics, or a digital certificate to confirm that the user is in fact the valid user and not an imposter.	

Business Issue	Suggested Action	Status
Some administrators set up accounts on network devices or the VPN that do not require secondary authentication. While normal users are required to use secondary authentication, the administrators are not. Often the account and password the administrators use have significant rights on the machines in the Extranet and the Intranet.	Ensure that the ability to log onto a Cisco device using port 80 is disabled. Also, ensure that all VPN and remote users coming into the E-commerce site are required to authenticate with a valid account, password, and secondary authentication.	
If clients and employees are not properly authenticated, then they may be able to gain access to the E-commerce site and the Intranet.	Ensure that an authentication server is in place to properly validate clients and users before they enter the network. Secondary authentication techniques should be required and enforced. No exceptions.	
Microsoft's Internet Information Services (IIS) has had many security issues in the past. A failure to install patches on a timely basis could result in the server being compromised.	If IIS is used, ensure that patches are installed regularly.	
Unprotected code on the web server could result in the server being defaced.	Ensure that all code is properly secured and up to patch level.	
Some organizations do not preplan for a computer incident. As a result, when an incident occurs, they are often unprepared for the public relations issues that often arise.	Prepare a series of press releases that are preapproved by the legal department. When an attack occurs and becomes public knowledge, issue the releases, emphasizing that the controls worked and the attack was limited by the control structure.	

(continues)

Business Issue	Suggested Action	Status
FTP is a very insecure service. Many E-commerce sites continue to use it to enable clients to download information and to transfer files to their E-commerce environment. It can also be used by hackers to store undesirable material or to run a sniffer on the E-commerce network.	FTP servers should not be used. If it is necessary to transfer files between trading partners and customers, use secure FTP.	
Some E-commerce sites use the "dump the data over the fence" technique to propagate client information to the E-commerce environment from the internal network servers or the mainframe. Also, client transactions may be stored on a server within the Extranet. This data may, if the server is compromised, be copied and disclosed by hackers or subject to accidental or intentional deletion.	It is better to have the web applications connect to the required Intranet machines through a secure connection. If this is properly implemented, there will be very little data in the Extranet for a hacker to harvest. Traffic between the Extranet and the Intranet should be encrypted.	
If the Internet and Intranet firewalls use the same technology, they could both be susceptible to the same exploits.	Use different operating systems as well as different firewall vendors on the Intranet- and Internet-facing firewalls.	
A failure to use a honey pot (a machine with known flaws that attracts hackers. When they attack the honey pot, a message is sent to the security officer that the system is under attack) could result in an undetected firewall penetration.	Where not specifically prohibited by law, use a honey pot to provide hackers with a target to attack. When the machines come under attack, generate an alert to the security officer or the web administrators.	

Business Issue	Suggested Action	Status
If the E-commerce site is subjected to a DoS or DDoS attack, then your customers and trading partners may not be able to access your site. Also, if any component in the E-commerce site fails, customers may be unable to perform transactions.	There should be a comprehensive, tested business continuance plan to ensure that your E-commerce site can detect a problem and automatically fail over to the secondary ISP and firewall.	
If a server in the Extranet fails, then critical transaction processing may be interrupted. This could cause serious customer service and trading partner issues as well as cause a public relations disaster.	Ensure that there are replicas of all critical servers in the Extranet. These servers also can be used for load balancing during peak processing hours.	
If a disaster occurs that destroys or disrupts your E-commerce site, then customers and trading partners may be affected. This can have a serious impact on your reputation and a potentially costly impact on your operations.	Ensure that there is a replicated configuration at a remote location. If possible, this should be a full replica of the original site so that it can take over on a moment's notice.	

AUDIT AND SECURITY CHECKLIST

No.	Question	Yes	No	WP XREF	REP XREF
1.	Is your E-commerce site secure?				
	a. Has it been tested by an independent third party?				
	b. Is it properly configured?				
	c. Are there controls in place to detect a serious hacking attempt?				
2.	Has your E-commerce site been divided into zones to properly protect your business assets?				
	a. Is there an Internet zone to defend the perimeter?				
	b. Is there an Extranet Zone that contains your E-commerce trading partner and customer access servers?				
	c. Is there an Intranet that contains your primary internal network assets (mainframe, etc.)?				
3.	Are the services and ports on the routers restricted to those that are safe and absolutely required?				
4.	Are the following services inactive on the routers?				
	ICMP (ping)?				
	a. Telnet?				
	b. Finger?				
	c. SNMP?				
	d. FTP?				
	e. TFTP?				
5.	Is there a strong community string on all network equipment?				

No.	Question	Yes	No	WP XREF	REP XREF
	a. Is it at least eight characters in length?				
	b. Does it contain special characters as well as alpha and numeric characters?				
	c. Is it changed on a regular basis?				
6.	**Were all firewall servers hardened before the firewalls were installed?**				
7.	**Was the firewall properly installed to ensure that it is secure and protects the environment?**				
	a. No unnecessary ports or services open?				
	b. No remote administration?				
	c. Root or administrative logins only permitted at the console?				
	d. Was the configuration reviewed by a specialist to ensure that it is properly configured?				
8.	**Have the firewall rules been carefully selected to ensure they provide the correct level of security?**				
	a. Were the rules approved by the chief security officer?				
	b. Were they carefully examined to ensure that they do not conflict with each other?				
9.	**Are there formal change management procedures in place over the firewall and over all machines used in E-commerce?**				
	a. Is there a provision for emergency patches?				
	b. Is an image copy taken before the patches are applied?				
	c. Are critical patches installed when security bulletins or emergency fixes are announced by vendors?				

(continues)

No.	Question	Yes	No	WP XREF	REP XREF
10.	**Is all activity on the firewall logged?**				
	a. Are there automated routines to identify serious issues and send alerts to the security officer and or the web administrators?				
11.	**Are all machines in the Internet and Extranet zones protected by the firewall or firewalls?**				
	a. Could any of the machines be compromised by hackers?				
	b. Could any of these machines be used as firebases by hackers?				
	c. Have any of these machines been compromised?				
12.	**Does management receive reports of computer incidents that were successfully blocked (number and severity)?**				
	a. On a daily basis?				
	b. On a weekly basis?				
	c. On a monthly basis?				
13.	**Is intrusion detection software in place?**				
	a. Is it properly tuned?				
	b. Could professional hackers defeat the effectiveness of the IDS?				
	c. Are false positives minimized?				
14.	**If UNIX machines are used, are the "R" services and other dangerous services disabled?**				
	a. Rexec?				
	b. Rlogon?				
	c. Rshell?				

No.	Question	Yes	No	WP XREF	REP XREF
	d. Finger?				
	e. Echo?				
	f. Chargen?				
	g. Smtp?				
	h. Verify?				
	i. Expand?				
15.	**Is the /.rhost file empty and secured with no read, no write, and no execute for the owner, the group, and the world?**				
16.	**Are all UNIX password files shadowed?**				
17.	**Is the cron file properly secured to ensure that normal users cannot view or change it?**				
18.	**Are all processes within the cron file secured so that normal users cannot read or write to them?**				
19.	**Is a VPN used to enable users to log in?**				
	a. Is strong encryption used?				
	b. Is secondary authentication used such as biometrics, digital certificates, or tokens?				
20.	**Are there any users who can bypass secondary login procedures?**				
	a. Administrators?				
	b. Security officers?				
	c. Others (please list)?				
21.	**Is there any way for an administrator or other user to log into routers, switches, or VPN and gain access to the Extranet or Intranet?**				

(continues)

No.	Question	Yes	No	WP XREF	REP XREF
	a. Are all network devices and firewall configurations reviewed on a regular, surprise basis?				
22.	**If IIS is used, is it at the current patch level?**				
23.	**Is all code on the servers properly protected? Could the web site be defaced through cgi or other poorly secured code?**				
24.	**Is your organization prepared for a computer incident?**				
	a. Is there a preapproved press package available for quick modification, then release?				
	b. Does it include a statement that the controls worked, which resulted in early detection (if this is true)?				
25.	**Have all FTP servers been removed from the E-commerce site?**				
26.	**Do customers have to authenticate to the Extranet servers or the authentication server before gaining access to their data?**				
	a. Is the data protected?				
27.	**Are different technologies used for the Internet-facing and Intranet-facing firewalls?**				
	a. Are the operating systems different as well?				
28.	**Is there a well coordinated and tested business continuance plan?**				
	a. Are several ISP connections used?				
	b. Are critical assets replicated?				
29.	**Is there a strong, proven, and tested disaster plan for the E-commerce application?**				

CHAPTER 6

Protecting E-Commerce Data

In the last chapter, the protection of your E-commerce site from the Internet was discussed. Unfortunately, no matter how strong your Extranet defenses are, it is always possible that a new exploit could defeat your best efforts to secure the web presence. If the controls fail, then other controls must kick in to protect and safeguard your internal data. Of great concern is that your confidential data will be compromised. Recently, several news stories about hackers breaking into systems and taking personal information have been reported. This information can be used to assume someone else's identity, to obtain credit cards, and even loans.

Identify theft is a booming and growing business with plenty of customers willing to pay to become someone else. A person with a criminal record or an illegal immigrant may want a new identity so that they can get a decent job. Terrorists may want passports so that they can enter the country. An estranged spouse may want a new identity to avoid paying alimony or support, and debtors may want to avoid paying their obligations. Whatever the reason for the new identity, there is a large market waiting to be filled. With this type of demand, it is no wonder that hackers are constantly probing networks looking for weaknesses. When they find poorly secured systems, they exploit them in the hope that they can penetrate the defenses and reach their goal, the personal information of your customers, clients, or business partners.

A common misconception is that this data is stolen from the Internet, making many people fearful of using the Internet. In fact, most electronic identity theft or the theft of financial information is not through the Internet. Rather, it is usually taken from servers on the inside of the network where it is often stored unencrypted. Once on a server, hackers or even your own employees seeking additional income can harvest data at will, normally without detection. Yet the perception that the Internet is the culprit prevails amongst most of the population. When a serious control incident occurs, it is easier to blame the Internet as the cause of the unauthorized disclosure than to admit that the internal network and server security is so poor that client information was stolen.

Let's assume that your firewalls are breached. When this occurs (not *if* it occurs), multiple defenses are necessary to protect your data and program files. Too often, when I investigate serious computer incidents, I hear the phrase "But we had a firewall." While auditors are often faulted for being overly control oriented, they are usually right. One has to assume that any control, even a firewall, can be beaten. Therefore, one of the basic premises of a strong structure of internal control is the concept of implementing a series of effective controls. If any one control fails, then other controls must come into play.

Unfortunately, many organizations do not understand the need for multiple layers of controls. I've heard the mantras so often that I can recite them in my sleep. "It won't happen here." "We need to have 17 people with administrator access in case the system fails at 3 A.M. on a holiday weekend." "We do not need application controls because the controls are in the database." "We do not need database controls because the controls are in the operating system." "The vendor software will not run on a server that has the current patches installed." "The vendor software will not run without trust relationships" (even though they create a massive security back door). My favorite is, "Security was never included in the original specification."

By accepting these justifications for poor control, you are preparing the way for hackers to compromise your network, servers, and the data on the servers. In my years as an auditor, I have heard many people refute internal control. Rather than acquiesce, I have always challenged these refutations. When someone says the vendor software will not run in a controlled environment, I call the vendor for confirmation. When I am told that software will not run on the current patch level, I ask them to install the patches on the test machine and rerun the acceptance test package. When I am told that the application will not run without trust relationships, I suggest that they try using TCP wrappers and secure socket layer to communicate between machines. After these suggestions, they usually hit me with, "I'm willing to accept the risk." If they say that, then I prepare a document for the audit committee, the CEO, and the chief legal officer outlining the specific risks that the person is willing to accept. I then request that the person who is rejecting controls and accepting serious control weaknesses sign and send this document. Because there are often Sarbanes Oxley implications, which I outline in writing, very few managers are willing to sign my document. Instead, they open their minds to create an acceptable control solution.

One of the first things I emphasize is that we must have multiple control structures in place. I always start with the entry points into the network. The first and most understood is the attack from the Internet. Here, the control is a strong defense consisting of several firewalls, intrusion detection software, and honey pots to attract the successful hackers. This will increase the likelihood of early detection. Another popular way to beat the network is through wireless access points. Here the control is to use Cisco Leap and RADIUS technology to create a secure, encrypted tunnel for your data. Also, be sure to test for rogue access points on a regular basis. (These items are covered in greater detail in Canaudit seminars and in past issues of the *Canaudit Perspective,* which are available at *www.canaudit.com/articles.*) For the purposes of building a secure E-commerce environment, I would like to build the defenses from the inside out, rather than use the traditional outside in methodology.

SECURING CONFIDENTIAL DATA

Let's start this process with the most critical item you want to secure, your confidential data. Data is the target of hackers and disgruntled employees or contractors. The first step in protecting your data is to classify it as public, confidential, or private information. I define public data as data that could be printed on the front page of the *Wall Street Journal* and the CEO would not be upset. Confidential data is data that should be protected from general distribution. This may include customer information, medical records, production data, or pricing information. Federal and state laws such as HIPAA (the Health Insurance Portability and Accountability Act of 1996), mandate that personal data be protected. The first way to protect it is to encrypt it when it is transmitted and when it is stored. Most of our clients understand the need for encryption during transmission; however, most think that encrypting stored data is going too far. Also, the cost of encrypting data is higher than not encrypting it. I believe that in a decade or so, data encryption will be commonplace. In the meantime, you may not want to fight the encryption battle in your organization. This does not mean that you should not classify your data, just that, in some cases, encryption is not an acceptable solution.

So, what can we do if encryption is not an option? Well, the first thing is to ensure that all databases and files are protected. Access permissions are generally available on your servers. These permissions break down one way or another into three basic groups. The first is the owner of the data, who can usually read, write, alter, delete, or execute the files. Users are often placed into groups and are able to access information available to that group. Normally this access would be restricted to the ability to read the data or execute the programs. In some cases, the group may need to write, alter, or delete the data or records within the data. The third set of users is what everyone or the "world" can do. These are people with a normal user or guest account on the system, who are not granted access by virtue of being the owner or a manager of a group. Everyone who accesses a system should only be able to read public data. They should not have the right to alter, delete, or write to the data, nor should they be able to harvest or steal confidential data.

If data is properly protected, then when the server is compromised with a normal user account, the damage will be limited to the access that the user has. By ensuring that nonpublic databases and files are not world readable, we are defeating the hacker, or unauthorized employee, or contractor's ability to easily steal information.

Right about now, I suspect that you are wondering how to determine if data is properly protected. This depends on the operating system, which in many cases is UNIX based. In the UNIX world, we run a simple command from the root directory (ls -albRF > /tmp/outputfile.txt). This produces a list of all of the file permissions. We load this into a Microsoft Access database, then run some preformatted queries. Two of these provide us with a list of the world readable and world writeable files as well as a count for world readable and writeable files. These are the files that can be harvested by a hacker or unauthorized employee, or in the case of world writable files, altered and changed using a normal account.

Using another query, we seek out the database files and the database backups (usually called exports). In most cases, the exports are world readable. Since we now know the location of this file, we can easily download it, just as a hacker would. All we have to do now is import the exported database into our own database and your data, including identity-related information, is our data.

There are two simple things you can do to prevent hackers from stealing the database in this manner. The first is to ensure that the database export can only be accessed by the owner or the database administrator group. There should be no world access at all. This will protect the export. To reduce the number of world readable files in the UNIX environment, set the umask (a parameter that defines the default file permissions when a file is created) to 027. Now when files are created, they will be better protected.

In the Windows environment, file permissions are normally set so that everyone can read, write, alter, and delete. This should be changed so that only the account holder or the group can access data. In the mainframe environment, access control software should be used in conjunction with database access controls to ensure that the databases are properly protected, both when the database is active and when the database software is not running. In many of our mainframe database audits, we found that the data is protected when the database application is running, but not when the database is shut down for backups or other reasons.

Once the data is secured, the next level of control is the database. While many of the controls are specific to a particular Relational DataBase Management Software (RDBMS), there are some generic things that can be done to improve control. The most important is to limit the accounts with DataBase Administrator (DBA) rights. Accounts with these powers can bypass most database and application controls. Worse, many DBA accounts have simplistic passwords. In addition, there may be default accounts with well-known passwords in your database. Using the Oracle RDBMS, examples of these accounts are SYS (password is change_on_install), and system (password manager). In addition, if you are running PeopleSoft or SAP in an Oracle environment, there are usually database access accounts that are used by the application software to access and update the database. The passwords for these accounts are rarely changed. If you want to find the password and you do not have DBA rights, simply scan the development Oracle server for SQL programs that have embossed passwords. I usually search for a data string of "passw." Once a hacker has the database access password, the databases and all data in them are easily compromised. There are many more control issues in the database environment. (If you require additional information, email *Gordon@canaudit.com* and request our Oracle audit and security guides.)

SECURING THE UNIX ENVIRONMENT

Once the data is protected, the operating system needs to be hardened to prevent hackers who penetrate the network from gaining access to the machine and then elevating their capabilities to root level using exploits. Sixteen things to do to protect the UNIX operating system are:

1. Ensure that all accounts have a password and that the password is not equal to the account name.

2. Ensure that trust relationships are eliminated. Seek out all copies of .rhost files, especially the root .rhost file, and remove them. Then create a blank .rhost file, place it in the root directory, and set the permissions to no read, no write, and no execute for the owner, the group, and the world. This will prevent a hacker from placing an .rhost file into the root directory and using that file to escalate their capabilities.

3. The hosts.equiv file can also be used to create a trust relationship. Empty this file and ensure that it is also properly protected.

4. In conjunction with items 1 through 3, disable the rlogin, rexec, and rshell services in the Inetd file. The administrators normally object to this because they say the software will not run. We suggest that

they use secure shell and TCP wrappers to create secure connections between servers. (This requires testing prior to implementation). The software vendor may need to be contacted to assist in this effort. Several of my clients have had difficulty getting the vendors to cooperate. Recently, we found a solution that makes the vendor realize that you are serious and that they have to perform. If the vendor states that the software will not run without trust relationships and they are unwilling to provide a solution in a reasonable time frame, have your general counsel send the CEO and chief legal counsel of the vendor a notice that their software is placing your environment at risk, that they were advised of this, and refused to provide a solution. Specify that should there be a subsequent computer incident relating to the use of trust relationships, then your organization will hold the vendor responsible. Further state that since the vendor was notified and refused to accept security principles mandating the elimination of trust relationships, the vendor may be deemed negligent because you provided them with prior knowledge of the risk and they refused to correct the problem or work toward a solution. Is this playing hardball? Yes, it certainly is. However, if your data is stolen because of a trust relationship and your customer data is compromised as a result, you can expect a class action suit. I don't think a jury of 12 of your peers would accept the excuse: "The vendor software would not run if the machine was properly secured." In fact, your organization may be held negligent and suffer treble damage as well as loss of reputation and customers.

5. Ensure that the TFTP service, which enables guests to connect to the system without authentication, is disabled. If TFTP is enabled, then all of the world-readable files will be accessible to unauthorized staff, contractors, or hackers and they will be able to freely download them. Also, world-writeable files could be altered or deleted using TFTP. Get rid of this service anytime you find it.

6. Some files contain processes that execute with root capability. The two I worry about the most are the inittab and the crontab. The inittab executes the processes within the inittab whenever you boot the system. The crontab contains processes that run at prespecified times. If the permissions on any of these files are world writeable, then a disgruntled user or hacker could alter the processes to create a new account the next time the processes are run. Therefore, check the permissions on all files in the inittab and the crontab to ensure that they cannot be accessed by low-level users or through TFTP. To launch a modified process in the crontab, you only have to wait until the scheduled task

runs at the appointed time. Then your process can recreate a new root-empowered account. For the inittab, the system must be rebooted. Therefore, launching a denial of service attack against the machine could force a reboot and the execution of the hacker's bogus code.

7. A simple denial of service attack can be launched by using two services together. Chargen generates characters and echo repeats them. By launching chargen and echo together, it is possible to cause the machine to busy itself creating characters and echoing them into an endless loop. Therefore, disable both of these services as they could be used to cause a reboot of the system that contains an altered inittab as described in item 6.

8. The next item is to ensure that the finger service is disabled. A hacker uses this service to identify accounts on the system. For example, if I finger a value of Gord and there is a gsmith account with the descriptor "Gordon Smith" in the comment field of the password file, then finger will tell the hacker that the account gsmith exists on the machine. By automating this process, a hacker can enumerate multiple accounts on the system, then guess passwords using a dictionary or brute force software tool to obtain a valid account/password combination.

9. The group file is used to assign user accounts to specific groups to give them the access required to perform their function. First, this file should never be world writable. Second, users in each group should be reviewed regularly to ensure that they do not have more access than they require.

10. The permissions file, if used, may contain entries that permit unauthenticated access to the system. The permissions file should be reviewed frequently to ensure that it does not contain unauthorized entries.

11. The systems file may contain a list of entries that include a server name or a phone number, an account name, and an encrypted password. These entries should be removed from the file to prevent hackers who compromise one machine from gaining access to another machine.

12. One of the most important controls is to ensure that account lockout is in place (normally, three bad passwords and the account is disabled). Also, bad passwords should be logged. If possible, an alert should be generated when there is a continuous flow of bad passwords against an account or a series of accounts. This fits the pattern of an automated or brute force password attack.

13. While it may sound foolish to again bring up changing passwords frequently, most UNIX machines I have audited do not require users

to change their passwords. Users with normal accounts should be required to change their passwords every 35 days or so. Empowered users, such as root or database administrators, should change their password more frequently or use secondary authentication techniques such as biometrics (iris scan), a token (SecurID), or a digital certificate.

14. The password for the root account should not be shared. If some users require root-like privileges, it is better to give them these privileges using the sudo function. If a user needs to do backups, we can give the user root access (bad idea) or we can use the sudo feature to grant them the ability to perform backups (good idea). Sudo is a public domain script that runs on most versions of UNIX.

15. UNIX security patches and fixes should be applied as soon after they are released as possible. I know that this increases the risk of the patch causing an operating system outage or application failure. However, this must be balanced with the risk that the hackers, upon hearing of a new exploit, will hunt down unpatched systems soon after the patches are released. Those who are tardy in implementing the patches may find their systems compromised.

16. Finally, the system logs should be reviewed frequently. For better control, create a software routine to scan the logs for occurrences of critical security issues. Then generate a page to the administrator's pager or cell phone so that they can take immediate action. Early detections will enable your organization to minimize the damage and possibly catch the perpetrator.

There are many other UNIX risks; however, the ones mentioned in this list are the most common. Review this list with your system administrators and assist them in obtaining management approval to implement them. After all, the operating system protects the data and the programs. Without strong controls, your data may be compromised or stolen. (If you need some UNIX audit and security scripts, visit *www.canaudit.com/downloads.*)

SECURING THE WINDOWS SERVER ENVIRONMENT

In the Windows environment, there are many security issues. Depending on which version you are running, security can be abysmal or it can be excellent. Windows NT is very easily compromised unless all of the vendor recommended patches are installed. The Windows 2000 server is better than Windows NT; however, it is still susceptible to many of the same control issues. The Windows

2003 server is a dramatic improvement over both of these operating systems. While I try not to make costly recommendations, the sooner you move to Windows 2003 and implement the stronger control structure that is available in that operating system, the sooner your data will be protected.

It is not just the servers that are at risk. Hackers love to go after workstations, as they are usually poorly controlled. I suggest that you immediately upgrade the workstations to Windows XP professional version. It is only a matter of time until you will have to upgrade the server and the workstation operating systems. You should bite the bullet sooner rather than later to properly protect your data and programs.

That said, let me take you through the process of testing (or hacking) security in the Windows environment. First, let me state that all of the tools I mention in this section are available on the Canaudit web site (*www.canaudit. com*). Just download them when you are ready to do your audit or security review. The first tool I use is Solar Winds, IP browser. This tool uses the Simple Network Management Protocol to scrounge information about the machines on the internal network. If it identifies a Windows 2000 or Windows NT with a default community string (public or private), at the click of a button, it will provide a list of all the account names on the server. Since there are often accounts that do not have a password or have a password equal to the account name, it usually does not take long to guess a valid account and password combination. An example of the data produced by Solar Winds IP Network Browser is:

```
# Subnet_xxx.xxx.xx.1___255.255.255.0.txt exported on 5/4/2003 6:14:50 PM
# IP Network Browser version 5.0.127

xxx.xxx.xxx.7 :
    Windows NT Domain Controller
    Community String: public
    Accounts
        Administrator
        alexander
        audrey
        bob
        gateway
        Guest
        mario
        Psoft
        support
        test
        TsInternetUser
```

Shares

SYSVOL
   Path: C:\WINNT\SYSVOL\sysvol
   Comment: Logon server share
mspclnt
   Path: C:\lolgistics\clients
   Comment:
NETLOGON
   Path: C:\WINNT\SYSVOL\sysvol\ezbroadnet.com\SCRIPTS
   Comment: Logon server share
Users
   Path: d:\users
   Comment:
Psoft
   Path: E:\Psoft
   Comment:

Not only do we now have accounts on this machine, but we know that PeopleSoft is installed on it because of the Psoft share and the Psoft account. But before we even try to guess any passwords, another tool, called ChkLock, is run. It displays the security settings on Windows 2000 and NT machines that have NetBIOS open and accessible to remote users. From a security standpoint, this tool enables one to quickly identify machines that do not have intruder lockout activated or that have inconsistent account and security policies.

F:\chklock>chklock xxx.xxx.xxx.7

ChkLock version 1.0a by Peyton Engel (pengel@berbee.com)

Minimum Password Length:	0 characters.
Maximum Password Age:	42 days.
Minimum Password Age:	passwords may be changed immediately.
Logoff Forced After:	users are not forced to log off.
Password Uniqueness Depth:	no password history is kept.
Lockout Duration:	30 minutes.
Lockout Reset Window:	30 minutes.
Lockout Threshold:	account lockout is turned off.
This machine's logon role:	primary domain controller.
The name of the PDC is:	
The name of the domain is:	HQMAIN

As you can see in the above example, there is no account lockout. Once a hacker is sure that they will not be locked out of an account, they can attempt to guess passwords. If the intruder is lucky enough to find a domain controller that does not have intruder lockout, he or she can then run NBTEnum against it. This tool will automatically determine if any accounts have no password or a password equal to the account name. It will also determine which accounts have administrator rights. If this is a hacker's lucky day, and it often is, he will find an administrator account and password. If not, he can attempt to brute force some of the administrator accounts.

If the servers are secure, then the hacker will run Cerberus Internet Scanner (CIS) or NBTEnum against a workstation. He may find a password for an administrator empowered account. Using that account, he will download the local machine password file and crack it. The target is the help desk account and password or another administrator empowered account and password that matches an account on the domain controller. Once he has that, he can simply log onto the domain controller and capture and crack the password file. When the cracking is complete, he then uses finger against the UNIX machines to find an account that is common between the Windows and the UNIX machines. After logging onto the UNIX machines with that account and password, a security Domino effect is set up, as the passwords cracked on one machine enable hackers to take control of other machines until they own the assets they want: your employee names, addresses, social security numbers, and other confidential information.

Network Issues

Once the operating systems are hardened, the next level of security is the network itself. (See also *Network Auditing: A Control Assessment Approach,* Gordon Smith, John Wiley & Sons, 1999, which covers this quite well.) In this book, it is necessary to cover the main points to ensure that the network and network devices protect the servers and the data. The most important control is to segment the network using routers, switches, or internal firewalls. Network segmentation, used properly, can restrict a hacking incident to a single network segment. This limits the damage that can be done when the network is penetrated and increases the likelihood that the intrusion will be detected in a timely manner.

That said, there are some key issues on the network side that must be addressed. One of my biggest concerns is that Simple Network Management Protocol (SNMP) will be active when it is not needed. If SNMP is enabled on your network, tools such as Solar Winds can be used to quickly document the network. Network equipment, servers, workstations, printers, and other devices that use a community string (SNMP password) can bleed information if the community string can be guessed or brute forced by Solar winds or other tools.

Many of our clients have a community string of public which enables us to see information such as account names, services running on the machine, and network routes that exist. With a community string of private, we can often download network device configurations which enables us to modify the configurations or worse, take control of the network devices. If you are using SNMP on the inside of your network, make sure that the community strings are complex (eight characters long, with a special character in positions 2 through 6). Also, the SNMP password should be changed on a regular basis, especially when there is network staff turnover.

Another control would be to set up a honey pot on the inside of the network. This will identify when a machine is scanned with a product such as Solar winds or Super Scan. I like a free tool called Back Officer Friendly which tells me when my box is being scanned. There are commercial versions of this product and other products that perform the same function. The point to remember is that normally an SNMP or port scan is one of the first things a hacker will do when they penetrate a network.

I love controls that are free because that often is the budget for network security. One of my favorite free controls is the ability to use router encryption to encrypt and decrypt data before it is transmitted across network segments. Encrypting this data prevents hackers and other nefarious people from sniffing accounts, passwords, or data off the network.

The next issue for discussion is external connections to the internal network. This includes modems, wireless connectivity, trading partner connections, and rogue Internet connections. Despite decades of warnings from both auditors and security professionals, we still find poorly secured modems, which I define as a modem that accepts inbound calls and permits repeated attempts to guess account names and passwords. In just about every network Canaudit has audited, we have found several poorly secured modems. Once found, we do the same thing a hacker would do. We scope the network access we have and identify poorly secured machines. Once that is done, we harvest passwords and crack them. It is a good day for the bad guys if they find a poorly secured version of PCAnywhere. (PCAnywhere is a great product; however, some people do not install it with the recommended controls, a strong account and password combination and encryption.) Once we are on a PCAnywhere machine, we can upload software such as network scanners and other attack tools. Once we fire them off, we can log off, and then come back in later to check the results. If this is done over a weekend, we can generally get a very good idea of the network map and attack the critical machines. Three simple controls will reduce the likelihood that PCAnywhere can be used in an unauthorized manner. The first is to ensure that accounts have strong passwords and intrusion detection is activated. When a hacker makes repeated attempts to guess passwords, PCAnywhere will disconnect them. If logging is turned on, then you will know someone has tried to guess passwords. (Only one control is listed.)

A Point-to-Point Protocol (PPP) connection is even better than PCAnywhere because it provides access to UNIX machines and network equipment. It is important that you seek out and find all modems, particularly those that are poorly secured. We use PhoneSweep from Sandstorm Enterprises as a war dialer. This product does an excellent job of finding modems and determining the operating system behind the modem. It also produces a distribution quality report. We suggest that war dialing be done once a month for small organizations and continuously for larger organizations.

Before putting modems behind us, I want to dispel any thoughts that modems are too slow to steal a large amount of information. One of our clients is a large regional bank that has Internet banking and statement distribution. We were able to bypass the firewall when we found a poorly secured modem. We connected to it and proceeded to download thousands of bank statements that contained a significant amount of confidential information. Yes, it took all weekend, but no one noticed until we showed the data to them at the end of the audit. Just because a modem is slow does not mean it is not an effective tool to compromise your E-business data.

Poorly secured wireless networks (especially 802.11b, the most common type) also pose a significant risk to your E-commerce data. On numerous occasions, I have sat in the parking lot of a client's facility and was able to access their network, sniff passwords, and harvest customer data. The wireless connections permitted me to bypass the firewall. Once onto the network, it does not take long to find web servers, Enterprise Resource Management (ERP) servers, and human resources information (just look for the Psoft or PSHR machine). Once onto these servers, we can download the data at speeds of up to 22 MBPS. Now through wider-fi (IEEE 802.16), which enables wireless access throughout a city or Metropolitan Area Network (MAN), we will see even greater growth in wireless communications.

My concern is not with the technology. My concern is that it has to be properly installed, secured, and managed. If someone is encrypting the signals with WEP (Wireless Equivalent Privacy), this is not strong encryption. Using a product such as AirSnort or Wepcrack, WEP can be cracked in minutes, once enough data is captured (usually 4 to 16 hours to trap enough data for the WEP keys to be cracked). I suggest your organization perform regular wireless sweeps to identify unauthorized and poorly secured wireless access points. Don't be surprised if you find that consultants working at your location are using it, or that users may set up their own wireless connections. Also, be careful of the newer laptop computers. Many of them come with wireless cards that may be activated. Once this machine is plugged into your network, it is possible that your internal data may be compromised.

Trading partner connections also can be an entry point. Often banks, investment firms, suppliers, and large clients are permitted to connect directly to your network. These connections are critical to ensure that business interactions flow smoothly and profitably. However, it is also necessary to ensure that the trading partners are restricted (using a firewall or network device filters) to the transactions they need to perform on the servers they need to access. Also, ensure that you are monitoring transaction volume or unusual increases in data traffic over the trading partner connection. If outbound traffic is increasing, then your data could be marching down the circuit, with your trading partner's network as a conduit.

Once your E-commerce data is secured, then the only component left to cover is the audit or security review of an application. Before moving on to the next chapter, take a few moments to review the risk/control table and checklists that follow.

DATA-RELATED RISK/CONTROL TABLE

Business Issue	Suggested Action	Status
Organizations that have not performed a data classification process to ensure that data is properly protected may be at risk of compromised or stolen data. Unless a data classification scheme/process is in place, users and programmers have no guidelines for determining how to protect resources. Customer information, including names, addresses, and social security numbers could be used for identity theft.	We recommend that management develop, approve, and promote the implementation of a data classification process. The process should identify and categorize all resources and define minimal protection based on risk, as follows: • *High Risk.* Information assets that would cause severe damage to the organization if disclosed or modified, personal and	

Business Issue	Suggested Action	Status
	medical data covered by various data protection acts, and employee information relating to disciplinary action are clearly in this class. Payroll, personnel information, and financial information about employees are also in this class because of the privacy requirements. • *Internal.* Source code, data, logs, etc. that would not expose the organization to loss if disclosed. • *Public.* Information that may be freely disseminated. All information resources should be labeled and protected according to the requirements set for each category.	
When the external Internet defenses are breached, the servers, data, and programs within the network are exposed to unauthorized access, information theft (harvesting of data), and the alteration and deletion of both programs and data.	Multiple control layers are required to properly protect E-commerce information. This includes the following items: • External and internal firewalls • Intrusion detection systems • Network segmentation • Discovery and security of modems and wireless connections • Implementation of network device, operating system, and circuit security	

(continues)

Business Issue	Suggested Action	Status
Data can be compromised if it is not properly protected. A failure to encrypt data during transmission through the internal and external networks can result in information theft.	Encrypt all data communications.	
Data can also be compromised when server security is breached. A failure to encrypt stored data could result in accidental or intentional information theft by hackers, disgruntled employees, or contractors.	Encrypt all confidential and private data on servers. Also, ensure that file permissions are set so that only the owner or the group can access the data.	
Databases and database exports may not be properly protected. As a result, hackers may be able to obtain a full copy database. If the database is not secure, they may be able to lift a copy of the export file from the server and import it into a database that they control, giving them a full copy of the information within the database.	Ensure that all databases, exports, and work files are properly protected. Also, conduct periodic scans of all file systems to identify and correct poorly secured data.	
If the file permissions on the database of the export are both world readable and world writeable, then the hacker can harvest the database, change the data, then overwrite the original file. If the export is altered, they can then use a denial of service attack to knock down the server and possibly force a recovery from the altered export file. This would install the hacker-originated changes into the production database.		

Business Issue	Suggested Action	Status
The more accounts that have DataBase Administrator (DBA) or similar access, the greater the risk that data can be compromised. Also, the organization is exposed to dueling administrator syndrome, where one administrator makes a change and another one changes it back to the original setting.	Restrict DBA access to those who perform the DBA function. Ensure that there are a limited number of DBAs.	
Some organizations copy data from the production environment into the development database so that they can test the new application. The development databases are normally not properly protected. In addition, developers often have greater rights than they require.	Live production data should never be used in a test environment. Programmers should not have DBA rights in the development databases. (See the Canaudit seminar "Control and Security of Oracle" for additional information.)	
Security in the Unix environment varies widely, as there is no common security standard across the environment. We often find that some systems were well secured, while others were not. These variances should be identified, and a standard baseline should be implemented.	The organization should develop a series of security standards to be applied throughout the Unix environment. At a minimum, the standard should address the issues identified later in this section: password strength, secure use of .rhosts files, elimination of .netrc files, reduction of trust relationships, and proper implementation of shadowed password files.

Management should approve the standards and ensure that they are enforced consistently across all machines. | |

(continues)

Business Issue	Suggested Action	Status
Most Unix machines have a large number of world-readable files. This is usually caused by setting the umask value to default (022). This results in an excessive number of world-readable files that can be viewed by any user or hacker who gains access to the network.	All public files (world-readable and -writeable) should be reviewed and secured. In addition, the umask should be set to 027 to protect against world-readable files.	
There are often .rhosts files on UNIX machines. Entries in these files create trust relationships that can be used to compromise other machines and give a hacker root access.	The .rhosts files should be removed. Then an empty .rhosts file should be set up in the /directory, with no access permitted to anyone other than root. This will prevent a hacker from replacing the /.rhosts file with one that grants the hacker root access. Trust relationships in host.equiv files should also be removed. If the trusts are required, then we recommend using the following in their place: • Implement the use of ssh (secure shell) in lieu of rlogin and rexec. This will encrypt the session from system to system and increase the authentication process by using a strong key. • Implement the use of tcp wrappers. This will restrict who can connect to the trusted systems, based on the source of the IP address.	
Most Unix machines are exposed to the "R" command exploits that enable hackers to gain root access to the system.	Rexec, rshell, and rlogin should be turned off. However, if it is necessary to run these services for a specific	

Business Issue	Suggested Action	Status
	application or other service, then these systems should be better secured. Suggested action: • Implement the use of ssh (secure shell). • Implement the use of tcp wrappers. This way, the trust relationships will stay in place, but the sessions will be secure.	
TFTP enables unauthenticated users to harvest world-readable files and alter or delete world writeable files on the system.	TFTP should be disabled.	
The SMTP service is often running on Unix systems and permits the use of the verify and expand commands. These commands enable hackers to identify the accounts that are on a machine without authenticating to the server. This gives hackers a better chance of cracking a valid account name and password and decreases the time to penetrate a system.	The verify and expand commands should be disabled on all SMTP running systems unless there is a proven need for this command to be activated.	
Some passwords used in the UNIX environment are very poor. Often they are defaults, blank, or the same as the account name. If a hacker can guess a valid account password combination, then they can get onto the system and harvest all world-readable files.	Force users to follow the password policy. Passwords should not be dictionary words; they should be eight characters in length and should have a special character in positions 2 through 6. Users should change their passwords on a	

(continues)

Business Issue	Suggested Action	Status
	regular basis (every 30 days). The Unix administrator should also crack passwords on a regular basis to ensure users are adhering to the policy.	
Often there are specific default accounts and passwords on a system (i.e., account oracle with a password of oracle). These passwords are often published in the manual or are available on the Internet. If a default account and password combination exists on a machine, then the machine and the data on it may be easily compromised.	Ensure default accounts and passwords are changed before placing the system into production.	
The finger service is often running on Unix systems. This service enables a hacker to gain valid account lists from systems without requiring authentication.	This service should be commented out in the /etc/inet/inetd.conf file.	
Occasionally we find that a .rhost file is world-writeable. This allows an attacker to set up a trust relationship to this system, then use it to gain root access.	The .rhosts files should be eliminated and replaced with an empty .rhost file. They should be readable only by root. The hosts.equiv files should also be root-readable only.	
Occasionally we find .netrc files on UNIX systems. These files can be very dangerous in that they store accounts and passwords in plain text.	Remove all .netrc files.	
Tools such as CIS and NBTEnum can be used to enumerate accounts on the	Wherever possible, the NetBIOS ports should be closed down. If NetBIOS must	

Business Issue	Suggested Action	Status
Windows NT and 2000 systems. The widely available tools use an unauthenticated null session to download share and account information from NT and 2000 systems. If a hacker is able to use CIS or NBTEnum against a poorly secured domain controller, then they may be able to discover valid accounts and passwords. If the hacker is truly fortunate, he or she will be able to glean a valid account name and password combination for an administrator empowered account, enabling them to download the encrypted passwords and crack them.	be used, then null sessions should be disabled. This can be changed via the system registry entry below: HKEY_LOCAL_MACHINE\System\currentControlSet\Control\Lsa add a dword entry: RestrictAnonymous = 1Alternatively. In the longer term, NT and 2000 servers should be replaced with Windows 2003. Windows 2000 and NT workstations should be replaced with Windows XP professional edition.	
Many passwords in the Windows environment are simplistic, both at a workstation level and a domain level. We normally crack about 70 percent of the passwords within 90 minutes. Ninety-five percent of the domain passwords were cracked in three days. Without strong password policies, a hacker may guess a valid account and password combination.	The password policy should be modified to include special characters. We recommend the following standard: • Passwords should be at least eight characters in length. • Passwords should have at least one or two special characters in positions 2 through 6. A good example is Ih8*#mice (I hate mice). • Passwords should be changed every 30 to 35 days. • All accounts with administrative rights should have the password changed every 15 days. • Another form of authentication should be	

(continues)

Business Issue	Suggested Action	Status
	looked into (like biometrics or smart cards). Management should ensure that every employee receives a copy of the security policy. Additionally, security training or briefings should be given to all users on an annual basis.	
Some of the new password crackers that are available on the Internet come complete with network sniffers. This enables the crackers to sniff encrypted passwords off the network as they are entered. Windows 2000 and NT provides the ability to restrict users to a specific set of workstations (up to eight). When workstation restrictions are in place, cracking a password does not grant access to the network unless the hacker is on one of the approved workstations or knows the name of the approved workstation.	Consider the use of workstation restrictions where applicable. In addition, especially for network administrators, consider the use of secure tokens, such as SecureID, for authentication instead of passwords.	
Poorly secured remote control software, such as PCAnywhere or VNC, can result in machines being compromised. Once compromised, data can be stolen, passwords can be cracked, and any existing sessions connected to other computers can be utilized by a hacker. In addition, if access software to the mainframe or other servers is available on	A remote access software policy should be created and strictly enforced. PCAnywhere is an excellent product and comes with free account and password authentication as well as the ability to encrypt sessions. We strongly suggest that these controls be implemented if PCAnywhere is used.	

Business Issue	Suggested Action	Status
the machine, then hackers may be able to connect to these environments.	Be wary of remote access software, such as VNC, that does not have strong encryption capabilities.	
If Windows 2000, XP, and NT Account Policies are not properly implemented, then the machines may be compromised, data may be harvested, and back doors may be placed on the systems.	Management should create standardized account policies. The administrators should periodically review account policies and ensure that they comply with the standard. We recommend the following settings: • *Maximum Password Age.* Determines when a user's password will expire. Passwords should expire every 30 to 35 days. The option of Passwords Never Expire should never be allowed. • *Minimum Password Age.* Limits the frequency of password changes. It prevents users, when coupled with Password Uniqueness, from using the same passwords over and over. It should be set to 1 day. • *Minimum Password Length.* Sets the minimum length of a password. Password length is an important factor in password-based security. Passwords should be at least 8 characters long. The option labeled Permit Blank Password should never be checked. • *Password Uniqueness.* This limits the user's ability to use	

(continues)

Business Issue	Suggested Action	Status
	the same password over and over. It should be set to at least 12 characters; however, 24 characters is much better. • *Account Lockout.* Locks out accounts after repeated logon failures. This should be set to three bad passwords within a 500-minute period. • *Forcibly Disconnect Users.* Forcibly disconnects users still logged on after lockout hours. This setting depends upon how the business functions. • *Logon to Change Password.* Determines whether users must log in to change their password. If setting is enabled, users must contact the administrator to change their password when it expires. This increases administration but improves security. We recommend its use.	
We often identify machines that have blank passwords, including the administrator or administrator-empowered accounts. Such poorly secured machines are an easy target for hackers.	A system of any kind should never be placed into production with a blank password, especially a blank administrator password on a Windows NT-based system. A basic security template for all Windows-based machines should be used. It should include the following: • Password Policy • Account Policy • Renaming of the Administrator account	

Business Issue	Suggested Action	Status
	• Replacing of the Everyone group with the Authenticated Users group on all hard drives installed • Disabling of remote registry administration in the registry • Disabling of the NETBIOS function if not being used (NETBIOS is not required for networks running strictly Windows 2000 and/or XP)	
The audit capability in the Windows environment provides excellent logging of control and security events. Failure to use this control mechanism or to install it properly could result in undetected machine penetrations.	There should be a standard Windows audit policy. We recommend the following audit settings: • Logon and logoff—audit failure. If the logs are manageable, you should also audit success. • File and Object Access—audit failure. If the logs are manageable, you may want to audit success. For example, this is where successful access to the SAM (Security Accounts Manager in Windows NT, XP 2000 and 2003) is logged. • Use of User Rights—audit failure. • User and Group Management—audit success and failure. • Security Policy Changes—audit success and failure. • Restart, Shutdown and System—audit success and failure.	

(continues)

Business Issue	Suggested Action	Status
	• Process Tracking—audit failure (optional).	
If the network is not properly segmented and secured, then when hackers penetrate the network, they have the ability to freely attack servers and network equipment throughout the network environment.	The network should be segmented to ensure that critical servers and information are protected. This can be achieved by either using internal firewalls or by using carefully configured routers with Access Control Lists (ACLs). By carefully constructing rule sets to enable permitted access to the required machines, the firewalled network segments will still be able to connect to the necessary business functions.	
Default community strings are being used with the SNMP service. This allows anyone on the network to gain useful information that would help in penetrating systems. It is also possible to harvest the passwords from network devices, such switches and routers.	The community strings should not have a default value. If SNMP is not being used, then disable this service. If SNMP is being used, change the community string to a hard-to-guess word. This will reduce the likelihood of someone guessing the community strings and gaining confidential information or gaining system access.	
If there are poorly controlled modems or wireless connections to the internal network, these connections could be compromised and used by hackers to bypass the external firewall. Once this occurs, they may have full access to the internal network.	Ensure that all modems and wireless network connections are properly secured. Also, perform regular modem and wireless searches to identify and mitigate poorly secured devices.	

CHECKLISTS FOR PROTECTING THE DATA

No.	Question	Yes	No	WP XREF	REP XREF
1.	**Has E-commerce data been classified?**				
	a. High risk?				
	b. Internal?				
	c. Public?				
2.	**Are multiple levels of controls used to create structured protection for the data?**				
	a. External and Internal firewalls?				
	b. Intrusion detection systems?				
	c. Network segmentation?				
	d. Discovery and security of modems and wireless connections?				
	e. Implementation of network device, operating system, and circuit security?				
3.	**Is data encrypted:**				
	a. When transmitted?				
	b. When stored?				
4.	**Is data protected so that only the owner and the group have access to it?**				
5.	**Are all databases and export files (copies) protected?**				
	a. Are any work databases removed after restoring databases?				
	b. Are periodic checks made to ensure that the databases, exports, and work databases are not world-readable or -writeable?				

No.	Question	Yes	No	WP XREF	REP XREF
6.	Are those individuals with DBA access and SYSDBA access limited to only those that absolutely require it?				
	a. Are there procedures to review the access of those with DBA or SYSDBA to ensure that they still require the access?				
	b. Are procedures in place to prevent "dueling administrators"?				
7.	Is the use of production data in the development databases prohibited?				
	a. Are the developers restricted to the development databases?				
	b. Are there several development DBAs so that programmers, analysts, and others do not perform DBA functions in the development databases?				

CHECKLISTS FOR UNIX SYSTEMS

No.	Question	Yes	No	WP XREF	REP XREF
1.	Are there standard secure builds for all machines involved in processing E-commerce transactions?				
	a. Internet-facing systems?				
	b. Internal systems?				
2.	Is the umask setting reviewed regularly to ensure that it is set at 027 and has not been changed?				

No.	Question	Yes	No	WP XREF	REP XREF
	a. Are there regular checks to ensure that world-readable and world-writeable files are minimized?				
3.	**Are .rhost files identified and removed?**				
	a. Is the /.rhost file emptied and secured with permissions equal to no read, no write, and no execute for the owner, the group, and the world?				
	b. Are secure shell and TCP wrappers used to enable safe communications once the /.rhost file has been secured?				
	c. Are the rexec, rshell, and rlogin features deactivated?				
4.	**Are host.equiv files emptied of all trust relationships and secured?**				
5.	**Is TFTP disabled?**				
6.	**Is FTP disabled and replaced with secure FTP?**				
7.	**Are the verify and expand commands disabled on simple mail transfer protocol?**				
8.	**Is the finger service disabled?**				
9.	**Are strong passwords used for all accounts?**				
	a. Passwords do not equal account name?				
	b. Passwords are not blank?				
	c. Passwords are not default values which are commonly known?				
10.	**Are periodic scans of the file system made to identify and remove all .netrc files?**				

CHECKLISTS FOR WINDOWS SYSTEMS

No.	Question	Yes	No	WP XREF	REP XREF
1.	Has the remote null session capability been disabled from all Windows NT and 2000 servers and workstations?				
2.	Do strong password policies exist?				
	a. Eight characters long or more?				
	b. Special characters in positions 2 though 6?				
	c. Passwords changed at least every 35 days or more frequently?				
	d. Secondary authentication such as tokens or digital certificates used where appropriate?				
3.	Are workstation restrictions used for critical accounts?				
4.	Is remote control software such as PCAnywhere properly secured?				
	a. Accounts and passwords?				
	b. Encrypted sessions?				
5.	Is the use of VNC and similar poorly secured products prohibited?				
	a. Are periodic scans made to identify versions of VNC?				
6.	Are account policies in use and do they meet or exceed the following standards?				
	a. Maximum password age set to 30 to 35 days?				
	b. Minimum password length set to 8?				
	c. Password uniqueness set to 24?				
	d. Account logout set for 3 back passwords in 500 minutes?				

No.	Question	Yes	No	WP XREF	REP XREF
	e. Accounts disabled until reset by administrator?				
7.	**Are periodic scans made to ensure that all accounts have passwords?**				
8.	**Is the audit function implemented?**				
	a. Are the values appropriate?				

CHECKLISTS FOR NETWORK ISSUES

No.	Question	Yes	No	WP XREF	REP XREF
1.	**Is the network segmented and secured?**				
2.	**Is SNMP activated?**				
	a. Are default community strings prohibited?				
3.	**Are all modems and wireless connections properly secured?**				
	a. Are periodic surprise checks made to ensure that modems and wireless connections remain properly secured?				
4.	**Has a full network audit been performed in the past year?**				

NOTE: If you need to do a full network audit, e-mail *Gordon@canaudit.com* for more extensive network checklists.

CHAPTER 7

Auditing an E-Commerce Application

Now that we have covered the technical aspects of E-commerce, it is time to address auditing an E-commerce application. When the Integrated Audit Approach was developed for Canaudit, I decided that auditing an E-commerce application should be performed in conjunction with the technical audit. For effective control to be in place, the Internet portal, the Extranet, the network, and the servers have to be properly secured. Database and application controls become the last line of defense and, as such, should be audited as part of the structure of internal control. At the start of the audit or security review (approximately 40 days before the start of fieldwork), you should issue the checklists for Chapters 2 through 6 of the book (the technical audit). In addition, you should issue the checklists from this chapter to the business application managers. Both groups should return them about 14 days before the fieldwork starts so that you can review them and prepare for the start of the onsite work.

Before proceeding to the audit guide from the Canaudit seminar "Integrated Auditing for Financial Auditors," let me explain our approach. The key concept is that we arrive at the client with a very good understanding of the application. We want to know what to expect, have a good idea of what surprises are in store for us, and we want to be fully prepared for any client questions. To achieve this objective, we anticipate the functionality of the application. We brainstorm the processes, controls, and risks and then create a series of audit checklists. We also determine the audit software tests we would like to perform. Keep in mind, this is just our expectation of the functionality of the actual application; we modify the audit guide as the audit progresses. At the end of the audit, our audit guide becomes our workpapers and parallels the application documentation (if there is application documentation).

This methodology enables the audit and security teams to be better prepared for the onsite work. By anticipating the application functionality and control structure, we ensure that we are knowledgeable about the application and have the correct tools to complete the project in an efficient manner.

Our process starts with an overview of the function. This enables us to determine the expected functionality of the application. Using this as a starting point, we break the functionality down into a series of processes and steps within the processes. This becomes the process analysis document. Working with the process analysis, we prepare a simple list of anticipated controls. Our risk assessment is developed concurrently, as the lack of a control usually creates a risk.

As always, I am worried about fraud, so our next step is to prepare the assessment of fraud potential. This, in conjunction with the risk assessment, helps us to prepare the audit checklists. The checklists are sent to the client about 40 days before the audit so that they can complete them at their leisure. This is a modified control self-assessment process, which I call cooperative auditing. While I do like the idea of control self-assessment, I prefer that the assessment be a joint effort between internal auditors or security analysts and the business unit staff. It takes a business unit manager to fully understand an application. A security analyst or auditor understands control structures. By working together, we can come up with a superior work product, far better than either group could do in isolation.

Once the checklists are complete, the risk/control tables are prepared. Again, these are initial risks. During the audit, we modify them as we get a more complete understanding of the application. When the audit is finished, we use the updated risk/control tables as the main body of our technical report. While management wants to know what the risks are, they are often more interested in cash flow. Therefore, we develop an audit segment for items with cash flow potential. We use this to sharpen our ability to recognize places where costs can be reduced and labor eliminated and, ultimately, where the audit group can have an impact on the bottom line. The last part of our application audit guide outlines some of the audit software tests we perform. Again, these are preliminary tests that will be expanded and refined as we complete the onsite audit work.

If you have any questions about the audit guide, feel free to e-mail me at *Gordon@canaudit.com*. Also, on the web site (see *www.canaudit.com*) that accompanies this book, there is an electronic copy of the audit guide. This will enable you to modify the guide to suit your particular environment. Based on past experience, most of our clients are able to use 75 to 90 percent of our original audit guide. Only 10 to 25 percent of the items need to be tailored to the client's particular environment.

SALES AND INVOICING FUNCTION AUDIT GUIDE

This module is intended to provide internal auditors with an integrated audit approach for the sales and invoicing function. Electronic commerce is now impacting both the sales and the invoicing functions. Customers have many options for ordering. They can have a salesperson call on them; they can use E-commerce to businesses and consumers; they can dial into the sales computer and place their order; or they can phone the order in. They can also order through CompuServe, America Online, or even through the Internet. This ordering flexibility provides new challenges for auditors because the implementation of new technology requires the implementation of new control techniques. Auditors must now audit both the paper and the electronic transaction trail. Also, electronic ordering poses new security threats such as network penetration, 800-line jamming, false orders, and use of stolen credit cards to pay for purchases.

   This module contains an overview of the sales and invoicing function and provides a detailed audit guide for readers to use in their audits. Most of the section is written in audit guide format to facilitate implementation of the integrated audit concept.

TABLE OF CONTENTS

1. Overview of the Sales and Invoicing Function

The world is changing rapidly as technology replaces the order-taking sales person with electronic order entry, business-to-business E-commerce, web pages, and order-by-modem or fax. Sales and marketing representatives, freed from the manual order-taking process, can now support the total needs of the customer and build long-term business relationships. This is necessary as customer loyalties, which used to be built on personal service, are being replaced by clients who want the best product at the best price. Quality, trading partner relationships, and cooperative marketing arrangements are now more important to the customer. Reducing the amount of labor required from the ordering process while improving ordering lead times and reducing inventory safety stock levels are as important as price and quality. An automated, efficient, and well-controlled sales and invoicing process is critical to the organization. Also, a zero tolerance for error attitude is required throughout the entire ordering and product delivery process.

A. Set-Up and Maintenance of New Accounts

New customers are critical to any business. It must be easy to set up a new customer, yet there need to be controls to ensure that the customer will pay for the goods ordered and that they comply with federal and state laws. Customer maintenance is required to process changes in basic customer information. Controls are required to ensure that goods are not diverted and that the invoice goes to the correct address.

B. Cash and Card Sales

Strong controls are required to ensure proper cash handling procedures and to reduce theft. Credit and debit card transactions are growing rapidly, as is card fraud. Controls are necessary to prevent errors as well as customer or staff fraud.

C. Sales Order Processing

It must be easy for customers to place orders. Various ordering technologies are available. Manual processing is very labor intensive and prone to error. Electronic order processing requires strong identification and authentication techniques to validate the customer. Also, strong edit routines are required to reduce errors and speed delivery of the goods.

D. Invoicing

The sooner an invoice is created and delivered to the customer, the sooner it will be paid. Electronic invoicing speeds the process and reduces labor. Manual invoicing may still be required for smaller accounts and those who resist automation.

Controls must be in place to ensure all goods purchased and shipped are invoiced and that the invoice is processed and sent to the client promptly.

E. Adjustments and Credit Processing

If there are errors in the invoicing or shipping processes, there will need to be adjustments or credits. Prices may be incorrect, items may have been lost or damaged during shipment, or the salesperson may need to match a competitor's price. These are all valid reasons for issuing a credit or an adjustment. However, these transactions could also be used to commit customer or sales staff frauds. Clearly, these items need to be monitored, not only for fraud, but also for quality and profitability reasons. Every credit or negative adjustment is a direct hit to the bottom line. A quality problem will have a serious impact on future sales and needs to be addressed quickly.

F. Returns

Returns are also a cost of doing business. They reduce profits and can erode customer loyalty. Returns are also highly susceptible to fraud. The salesperson may have placed the order to meet quota in one month, knowing the goods would be returned in the next month. Also, the customer may be returning goods that were used or were damaged by the customer. Strong controls are required over returns to ensure that goods were truly returned and that the reason for the return is identified.

G. Promotional Programs

Sales promotions include special discounts, allowances, cooperative advertising, rebates, and bonus products such as twofers (two for one), BOGOs (buy one get one free) and free product (25 percent more free). They are needed to promote the product; however, these programs must be controlled and monitored.

H. Customer Service

There is only one kind of customer service—good service. The customer requires prompt attention from courteous staff. If customers do not get good service from your organization, they will get it from your competitor.

I. Fraud Triggers

There must be strong preventive, nondiscretionary controls in place to reduce the exposure to fraud. But, remember the saying, "Where there is a will there is a way." Therefore, the system must also have detective controls such as fraud software or management reporting to highlight possible fraudulent transactions. We call the items that indicate a possible fraud a fraud trigger. The software used to report the triggers are called fraud sniffers.

2. The Audit Guide

This audit guide is provided to assist with the planning phase of the audit. It is intended to be tailored by the client, using the Word file provided as part of the material. The audit guide contains the following components:

A. Process Analysis

This is a detailed listing of the processes that may be present in this function.

B. Anticipated Controls

This is a listing of the controls we expect to find in this application.

C. Risk Analysis

The risk analysis is intended to identify specific high-level risks that are normally found in the application. It should be modified based on your own risk analysis.

D. Potential for Fraud

This identifies some of the frauds that could occur in this function. It can be used to design fraud triggers and fraud sniffers.

E. Checklists

These are sample checklists for you to use in your audit. They should be modified to your environment and sent out to the client approximately 40 days before the start of the audit.

F. Risk/Control Tables

These tables outline the specific risks of the application and suggest possible controls. They can be used in conjunction with the checklists to write the audit report.

G. Cash Flow Potential

This section is a list of items that may improve the bottom line.

H. Audit Software Tests and Specifications

This section contains a list of audit software tests and specifications for some of them. The forms can be used to create the basic audit software you require.

A. Process Analysis

PROCESS ANALYSIS FOR SET-UP AND MAINTENANCE OF NEW ACCOUNTS
Completed by: **Date:**   **Page of**

Office Originated New Account

Customer Walk-In New Account

1. Customer enters office to open new account.
2. Customer Service Representative (CSR) listens to customer's needs.
3. Customer information (name, address, etc.) is entered into new customer screen.
4. File is searched to determine if customer had previous accounts and the status of those accounts.
5. Customer credentials are verified.
6. New account application, such as credit history, required credit limit, and estimated purchases, is completed.
7. Initial order is taken and processed if a cash or card sale.
8. If the initial order is to be invoiced or paid by check, the order is placed on hold until the credit manager approves credit.
9. A sales representative is assigned to the account.
10. Customer is welcomed as a new customer.

New Business-to-Business E-Commerce Account

1. Either the customer or the company initiates negotiations to conduct business electronically.
2. A trading partner agreement is signed.
3. Agreements on types of transactions, transmission windows, and responsibilities are included in the trading partner agreement.
4. Electronic service provider information and addressing is shared.
5. Test transactions are processed by each side.
6. Once tests are proved, both parties go live.
7. Transactions are monitored until a proven track record is established.

(continues)

PROCESS ANALYSIS FOR SET-UP AND MAINTENANCE OF NEW ACCOUNTS

Completed by:	Date:	Page of

New Electronic Account

1. Customer logs onto web page.
2. Selects new account option.
3. Prompted to enter critical customer information.
4. Information is verified online via a credit bureau.
5. Customer views information on the various products and services offered.
6. Customer places first order. It is shipped if the customer has a valid credit card and the card issuer authorizes the charge.
7. If first order will be invoiced or cash on delivery, the order is placed on hold until credit manager approves credit line.
8. A sales representative is assigned to the account.
9. Customer is welcomed as a new customer.
10. A credit application/confirmation is mailed to the customer for signature.

Telephone New Account

1. Customer calls sales hot line.
2. Customer asked to provide critical customer information which is entered by CSR.
3. Information is verified online via a credit bureau.
4. Customer places first order. It is shipped if the customer has a valid credit card and the card issuer authorizes the charge.
5. If first order will be invoiced or cash on delivery, the order is placed on hold until credit manager approves credit line.
6. A sales representative is assigned to the account.
7. Customer is welcomed as a new customer.
8. A credit application/confirmation is mailed to the customer for signature.
9. A sales representative is assigned to the account.

PROCESS ANALYSIS FOR SET-UP AND MAINTENANCE OF NEW ACCOUNTS

Completed by:	Date:	Page of

Sales Representative Originated New Account

1. Sales Representative (SR) visits new customer and determines customer's needs.
2. Enters customer data into a notebook computer and transmits to head office through an encrypted VPN (Virtual Private Network) connection to the Internet.
3. May also take critical information on paper if SR uses manual customer origination and ordering.
4. New account application, including credit history, required credit limit, and estimated purchases, is completed.
5. Initial order is taken and processed if a cash or card sale.
6. If the initial order is to be invoiced or paid by check, the order is placed on hold until the credit manager approves credit.
7. Customer is welcomed as a new customer.
8. A credit application copy/confirmation is mailed to the customer for signature.

New Account Process, Back Room

1. Customer information is verified by credit report if not already completed.
2. Search is conducted to see if customer has other accounts. If so, the new account is linked to the other accounts in the customer database.
3. Search is conducted to see if customer has any unpaid invoices, or a history of high returns or credits.
4. Confirmation prepared and sent to client.
5. For electronic and telephone new accounts, new account package printed and sent to client for verification.
6. If credit check indicates customer is good risk, first order is released for shipment.

(continues)

New Account Process, Back Room (Continued)

7. Welcome letter sent out, along with marketing items such as catalogs.

8. Two weeks after new account is opened, customer service letter is sent to customer.

Maintenance

Name, Address, and Other Normal Changes

1. Customer notifies company of change by:
   - Phone
   - In person
   - By mail
   - Electronically

2. Customer is authenticated if in person, phone, or electronic transaction.

3. Mailed change is verified by phoning customer.

4. Changes to ship-to and invoice addresses are confirmed with a known contact.

5. Change is made.

6. Account is flagged to be watched for unusual transactions or activity.

7. Address changes are confirmed to old address with DO NOT FORWARD, return to sender, address correction requested.

8. Confirmation is also sent to customer by mail.

Closed Account, Customer Initiated

9. Customer is authenticated.

10. Reason for closing established.

11. Attempts to remedy problems taken to prevent closing.

PROCESS ANALYSIS FOR SET-UP AND MAINTENANCE OF NEW ACCOUNTS		
Completed by:	**Date:**	**Page of**

12. Check made to determine if any unpaid balances are outstanding.

13. Payment arrangements are made.

14. Close out account (save required government information and historical data).

15. Send out customer service questionnaire to customer.

Closed Account, Company Initiated

16. Customer is notified of the reason for closing the account by SR, CSR, or sales manager.

17. Decision is made on which orders, if any, are to be processed.

18. Account is flagged as closed.

19. No new orders are accepted.

20. Customer information is retained and a flag is set to ensure that the customer will not be able to open new account without credit manager involvement.

PROCESS ANALYSIS FOR CASH AND CARD SALES

Completed by:	Date:	Page of

Cashier Start-Up Routine

1. Cashiers receive cash drawers with standard float or previous day's balanced cash.
2. Cash is recounted and amounts verified.
3. Cashier logs on to cashier or POS station, using password and challenge response.
4. Supervisor enters authorization to validate cashier and activate cashier session.
5. Cashier float is entered.
6. Cashier accepts first customer.

Cashier-Based Customer Processing

1. Customer selects goods or picks up will call orders.
2. Cashier scans/tallies/writes up customer order.
3. If customer paying by cash, then is accepted (may be placed on top of cash drawer until after change is made).
   ➤ Change is made and given to customer.
4. Checks are verified:
   ➤ Numbers and figures agree.
   ➤ Account is not in hot card lookup file.
   ➤ Not stale dated.
   ➤ Customer ID requested and verified.
   ➤ Name and address on check cross-checked with customer's ID.
   ➤ Supervisor may be called over for approval.
5. If payment is by ATM card, card is swiped by customer who then enters PIN:
   ➤ System connects to bank and verifies funds.
   ➤ If there are insufficient funds, customer is asked for another form of payment.

PROCESS ANALYSIS FOR CASH AND CARD SALES		
Completed by:	**Date:**	**Page of**

> ➤ If no other acceptable form of payment (cash or credit card), sale is canceled.
> ➤ If there are funds for the transaction, the customer's account is debited and the company account is credited.

6. If payment is by credit card, system (or cashier) calls bank and requests approval for the amount of the sale:

> ➤ If approval is given, sale documents are prepared and signed by customer.
> ➤ If the transaction is declined, customer is asked for another acceptable form of payment (cash, ATM card, or another credit card).

Cash Pick-Up/Drop-Off

1. When cash amounts approach or exceed limits, computer initiates cash pick-up (or supervisor initiates if manual).
2. Pick-up screen/form is generated and initialed by cashier and supervisor (or PIN entered).
3. Manual log is also completed and initialed.
4. For cash drop-off, screen is opened, PIN entered by supervisor and cashier, manual log also completed and initialed by cashier and supervisor.

Cashier End of Shift

1. Shift summary is printed.
2. Cashier balances cash, checks, etc.
3. Cashier reconciles to shift summary.
4. If out of balance, differences are reconciled.
5. Supervisor also balances cash and reconciles transactions.
6. Cash is removed.

(continues)

PROCESS ANALYSIS FOR CASH AND CARD SALES		
Completed by:	**Date:**	**Page** **of**

Cashier End of Shift (Continued)

7. Drawer is filled with standard float and locked in vault by cashier and supervisor.

Supervisory Procedures

8. Over and short report is produced and reviewed by supervisor.
   - Significant items reviewed with cashier.
   - If fraud is suspected, security is notified.
9. Head cashier's daily sales/cash report is prepared.
10. Deposit is prepared and taken to bank or placed in safe for armored car pick-up.

PROCESS ANALYSIS FOR SALES ORDER PROCESSING

Completed by:	**Date:**	**Page** **of**

Gathering the Transactions for Batch Processing

Manual Transactions (Online Data Entry, Batch Update)

1. Sales orders are received from the salesperson or mailed or faxed by the customer.
2. Sales orders are taken over the phone by CSRs.
3. Sales orders are keyed by CSRs.
4. Transactions are edited to ensure critical data is correct:
    - Customer name
    - Customer number
    - Phone number
    - Bill-to address
    - Ship-to address
    - Delivery date
    - Product codes
    - Quantities checked against previous day's ending inventory balance to see if enough is in stock
    - Terms
5. Any errors detected are flagged and followed up.
    - For phone orders, the customer is notified during the call of any items that appear to be incorrect.
    - For faxed orders, the customer is called or faxed.
    - For SR originated orders, the SR is notified and contacts the customer; a CSR may also contact the customer.
    - Correction is entered and re-edited.
6. For out-of-stock items, the customer is notified that the goods have been placed on back order and the expected delivery date.
7. Order forms and faxed orders are batched by CSR.
8. Batches are balanced and reconciled, then stored in the pending order file.

(continues)

PROCESS ANALYSIS FOR SALES ORDER PROCESSING

Completed by:	**Date:**	**Page of**

Gathering the Transactions for Batch Processing (Continued)

9. For phone orders, the calls are recorded for customer service and accuracy.
10. Once the phone order is complete, the customer is given an order reference number for tracking purposes.

B2B (Business-to-Business) Transactions

1. The B2B service provider or the third-party service bureau is called, mailbox is opened, and transactions are retrieved.
2. Optionally, the client logs into the vendor's web site and initiates the transaction.
3. Transactions are sorted by B2B record type and fed to the correct system.
4. Transactions are edited and any transactions with errors are:
   - Rejected from the processing run.
   - Reviewed to ensure that it is not a system error.
   - Sent back to the customer as an error message.
5. Transactions are converted to internal record format, batched, and stored in the pending order file.

Web and Order-by-Modem Transactions

1. Customer logs in and is identified and authenticated using account name and password.
2. Customer views electronic catalog.
3. Customer selects items and quantities desired.
4. Inventory check is performed to determine if the goods are in stock.
5. Billing information is entered.
   - If credit or debit card, order is priced, card is validated online, and charged for the correct amount.

PROCESS ANALYSIS FOR SALES ORDER PROCESSING

Completed by:	Date:	Page of

➤ If customer is to be invoiced, account status is checked in A/R and if okay, order proceeds.

➤ If customer is paying C.O.D. or by check, past payment history and hot check file is checked; if okay, order proceeds.

6. Order is included in a batch and is placed in the pending order file.

Batch Order Processing (Daily or Several Times Daily)

---

1. Batches are read from the pending order file.

2. Transactions are edited and batches are balanced.

3. Batches with errors are rejected and placed in order error file for review and correction; corrections are reentered for next processing run.

4. For each order:

➤ The destination of the order is checked.

➤ The shipping point is determined based on location.

➤ Inventory at the shipping location is checked.

➤ If items are in stock, inventory on hand is reduced by order quantity.

➤ If items are not in stock:

• Inventory at other locations is checked.

• Open purchase orders are checked to determine if goods will be arriving soon.

• Item is either shipped from other location or placed on back order until goods arrive.

• Outstanding purchases arrive.

➤ Orders are prepared and routed to the warehouse or shipping location.

➤ Orders may be printed in the warehouse to enable goods to be selected.

➤ Orders may be distributed electronically to handsets carried by order fillers.

(continues)

PROCESS ANALYSIS FOR SALES ORDER PROCESSING

Completed by:	Date:	Page of

Batch Order Processing (Daily or Several Times Daily) (Continued)

- ➤ Shortages are recorded and routed to the invoicing area so an adjustment can be made.
- ➤ Goods are shipped.
- ➤ Shipping notice is sent to invoicing (if goods are invoiced on shipment).
- ➤ B2B order confirmation is sent to customer via B2B service provider for B2B transactions.

5. Once goods are shipped, open order is removed from open order file and archived.

Immediate Online Order Entry

Manual Transactions (Online Data Entry, Batch Update)

1. Sales orders are received from the salesperson or mailed/faxed by the customer.
2. Sales orders are taken over the phone by CSRs.
3. Sales orders are keyed by CSRs.
4. Transactions are edited to ensure critical data is correct.
   - ➤ Customer name
   - ➤ Customer number
   - ➤ Phone number
   - ➤ Bill-to address
   - ➤ Ship-to address
   - ➤ Delivery date
   - ➤ Product codes
   - ➤ Quantities checked against previous day's ending inventory balance to see if enough is in stock
   - ➤ Terms

PROCESS ANALYSIS FOR SALES ORDER PROCESSING		
Completed by:	**Date:**	**Page of**

5. Any errors detected are flagged and followed up.
   - ➤ For phone orders, the customer is notified during the call of any items that appear to be incorrect.
   - ➤ For faxed orders, the customer is called or faxed.
   - ➤ For SR originated orders, the SR is notified and contacts the customer; a CSR may also contact the customer.
   - ➤ Correction is entered and re-edited.
6. For out-of-stock items, the customer is notified that the goods have been placed on back order and the expected delivery date.
7. Completed orders are processed (see online order processing).
8. Order forms and faxed orders are batched by CSR for archiving.
9. For phone orders, the calls are recorded for customer service and accuracy.
10. Once the phone order is complete, the customer is given an order reference number for tracking purposes.

Web Transactions

1. The vendor or third-party service provider is called, mailbox is opened, and transactions are retrieved.
2. Transactions are sorted by record type and fed to the correct system.
3. Transactions are edited and any transactions with errors are:
   - ➤ Rejected from the processing run.
   - ➤ Reviewed to ensure that it is not a system error.
   - ➤ Sent back to the customer as an error message.
4. Transactions are converted to internal record format and forwarded to the online order processing system for immediate order preparation.
5. Order and transaction totals are developed and retained for automated reconciliation to the order processing function.

(continues)

PROCESS ANALYSIS FOR SALES ORDER PROCESSING		
Completed by:	**Date:**	**Page of**

Immediate Online Order Entry (Continued)

Web and Order-by-Modem Transactions

1. Customer logs in and is identified and authenticated using account name and password.
2. Customer views electronic catalog.
3. Customer selects items and quantities desired.
4. Inventory check is performed to determine if the goods are in stock.
5. Billing information is entered.
   - ➤ If credit or debit card, order is priced, card is validated online, and charged for the correct amount
   - ➤ If customer is to be invoiced, account status is checked in A/R and if okay, order proceeds.
   - ➤ If customer is paying C.O.D. or by check, past payment history and hot check file is checked; if okay, order proceeds.
6. Order is transferred to the online order processing module, the order is processed, and the customer is notified of the delivery date.
7. The order may also be invoiced at this time, with the invoice going back to the customer.

Online Order Processing (Continuous Process)

1. Items are received electronically from the originating order entry process.
2. Transactions are edited to ensure they were properly received.
3. Items with errors are rejected and an error message is sent electronically to order entry point for immediate resolution.
   - ➤ For manual data entry, error report is generated and sent back to the entry station for resolution.
   - ➤ The transaction and error are placed in order error file for review and correction; corrections are reentered for next processing run.

PROCESS ANALYSIS FOR SALES ORDER PROCESSING

Completed by:	**Date:**	**Page of**

4. For each order:
   - ➤ The destination of the order is checked.
   - ➤ The shipping point is determined based on location.
   - ➤ Inventory at the shipping location is checked.
   - ➤ If items are in stock, inventory on hand is reduced by order quantity.
   - ➤ If items are not in stock:
     - • Inventory at other locations is checked.
     - • Open purchase orders are checked to determine if goods will be arriving soon.
     - • Item is either shipped from other location or placed on backorder until goods outstanding purchases arrive.
   - ➤ Orders are prepared and routed to the warehouse or shipping location.
   - ➤ Customer is notified that order has been transferred to shipping location for selection and shipping.
   - ➤ Orders may be printed in the warehouse to enable goods to be selected.
   - ➤ Orders may be distributed electronically to handsets carried by order fillers.
   - ➤ Shortages are recorded and routed to the invoicing area so an adjustment can be made.
   - ➤ Goods are shipped.
   - ➤ Shipping notice is sent to invoicing (if goods are invoiced on shipment).
   - ➤ B2B order confirmation is sent for B2B orders.
5. Once goods are shipped, open order is removed from open order file and archived.

PROCESS ANALYSIS FOR INVOICING		
Completed by:	**Date:**	**Page** of

NOTE: Invoicing may already be performed if the sale was POS (Point of Sale), credit, or debit card. Invoicing can occur at point of original entry, several days before goods are shipped, or after goods are shipped.

1. Orders are received by the invoicing module from the order entry point if immediate invoicing is performed.

2. For invoicing several days before shipping, orders to be invoiced are extracted from the open order file.

3. For orders that are invoiced after shipping, the shipping documents are received (and entered, if manual).

4. The customer's price category and terms are extracted from the customer file.

5. For each item:
   - The price for the item in customer's price category is retrieved.
   - The quantity is multiplied by the price and the total is produced.
   - The total of goods ordered is created.
   - Taxes are computed and added.
   - Shipping charges are computed and added.
   - The invoice is created and sent to the customer:
     - By transaction to service provider
     - By e-mail to web and shop-by-modem customers (receipt requested)
     - By mail for paper-based customers

6. A reconciliation between items ordered and items invoiced is performed to ensure all ordered and shipped goods are invoiced.

7. Sales commissions, if any, are calculated and sent to payroll system.

8. The invoice is transferred to the A/R system.

9. Sales taxes by state are accumulated and transferred to the payables system.

10. General ledger is updated with the sales, taxes payable, commissions, etc.

PROCESS ANALYSIS FOR ADJUSTMENTS AND CREDIT PROCESSING		
Completed by:	**Date:**	**Page** **of**

Adjustments

1. Adjustments are gathered by type and source.
   - Shipping adjustments are retrieved from warehouse.
   - Pricing adjustments are input from CSR or SR.
2. Pricing adjustments are reviewed by sales manager to ensure they are valid.
3. Adjustments are transferred to the invoicing system for processing.
4. Reports are created for management, summarizing the adjustments by type and providing trend information.
   - Customers short-shipped goods. (The quantity shipped is less than the quantity ordered by the customer.)
   - Total price adjustments by SR and by customer.
5. Action is taken to identify the cause of the adjustment and to correct it.
   - Inventory cycle count to correct quantity on hand.
   - Ensure customer is in the correct price category.

Credit Notes

1. Credit note is prepared by SR based on customer complaint:
   - Damaged goods
   - Pricing errors
   - Shortages upon receipt, etc.
2. Credit note is entered into the system.
3. Credits resulting from shipping errors or damaged goods are sent to shipping point for review and approval.
4. Credits for matching competitor's pricing are sent to sales manager for review and approval.
5. Credits are tracked by customer to see if there are any significant trends.

(continues)

PROCESS ANALYSIS FOR ADJUSTMENTS AND CREDIT PROCESSING		
Completed by:	**Date:**	**Page of**

Credit Notes (Continued)

6. Some credits will be rejected and the SR will be notified.
7. Approved credit notes are transferred to the invoicing function for crediting the account.
8. Credits are consolidated and a series of management reports are created.
9. Cost of credits is compiled and trend analysis is performed.
10. If credit is for poor quality, the quality control system is updated with the transaction.

PROCESS ANALYSIS FOR RETURNS

Completed by:	**Date:**	**Page of**

1. Items are returned from the customer.
2. The reason for the return is determined:
   - ➤ Customer did not like product.
   - ➤ Product did not perform as desired.
   - ➤ Product is damaged.
   - ➤ Product was not ordered.
   - ➤ Product was not received on time, etc.
3. Returned product is inspected to determine if it is damaged.
4. Check is made to ensure there was no previous adjustment or credit for this item.
5. Decision is made to accept returned goods.
6. Credit note is created for approved credits.
7. Credit is transferred to the invoicing system for processing.
8. For cash sales, customer's money is refunded.
9. For credit and debit card sales, customer's original card is credited.
10. Management reports are produced for returns, by product type and reason code.
11. For products with high returns, action is taken to improve the product or to replace it with higher quality product.

1. Promotion programs are created by the marketing group.
2. Promotions involving packaging changes (BOGOs, bonus packs, etc.) are sent to engineering for product design and modification of the manufacturing process.
   - Volume is estimated.
   - New packaging is ordered.
   - Changes are made to the machinery and processes.
   - New UPC code is created and registered for the product (to prevent twofers being returned as onefers).
   - Product is produced and shipped.
3. For special discounts and allowances:
   - Terms and conditions are created.
   - SRs are briefed on the program.
   - Customers are contacted to participate.
   - Special contracts are created.
   - Special prices are entered into the invoicing system.
   - Orders are placed.
   - Special production runs are completed.
   - Product is shipped.
4. For cooperative advertising programs:
   - Special contract is designed and signed by both parties.
   - Proof of advertising is sent in by customer with invoice.
   - Ad is reviewed and invoice approved or declined.
   - If invoice is approved, credit is placed into the invoicing system for processing.
5. For rebates, customer sends in proof of purchase and an invoice.
   - Recent purchases are checked to ensure the customer purchases sufficient product for the amount of rebate requested.
   - Rebate invoice is approved and credit is generated in the invoicing system.

PROCESS ANALYSIS FOR CUSTOMER SERVICE

Completed by:	**Date:**	**Page** **of**

1. Customer service surveys are sent out for:
   - ➤ New accounts
   - ➤ Closed accounts
   - ➤ Periodic random sample
2. They are returned to an outside service, keyed into the system, and evaluations are produced.
3. Customer service reports are produced and reviewed by management.
4. Service quality is monitored to identify improvements or degradation of service levels.
5. Management takes action to improve customer service.

B. Anticipated Controls

ANTICIPATED CONTROLS FOR NEW CUSTOMERS		
Completed by:	**Date:**	**Page of**

1. All new customers should be identified.
2. Customer should complete new account application or sign contract:
   - ➤ Manually
   - ➤ Online
   - ➤ On the web or shop-by-modem
3. All required information should be presented and edit routines should be in place.
4. Customer information should be verified against a database.
5. Credit check should be performed for accounts to be invoiced.
6. Initial deposit may be required for some accounts.
7. Customer should be given information on using B2B and other automated ordering and payment techniques.
8. Customer information should be confirmed to the customer.
9. A Sales Representative (SR) should be assigned to the customer.
10. New customer survey should be sent to the customer.

ANTICIPATED CONTROLS FOR PROCESSING CUSTOMER TRANSACTIONS

Completed by:	Date:	Page of

1. Cashiers should count cash and negotiable instruments at beginning of shift.
2. Supervisor should verify count.
3. Cashier should use account name and password to log into system.
4. Supervisor should validate cashier.
5. Customer should be identified and authenticated.
6. Cash should be counted and verified.
7. Checks should be reviewed for completeness and accuracy before negotiation.
8. Cashier floor limits should be used.
9. Supervisors should approve all transactions over the floor limit.
10. Cash should be picked up from cashier on a regular basis or when cash on hand exceeds prespecified limit.
11. Cash pick-up and drop-off should be recorded in system and on a separate log.
12. Cashier and supervisor should enter PIN or initial form to authenticate transaction.
13. Cashier should balance at end of shift.
14. Supervisor should review balancing.
15. Out-of-balance conditions should be reconciled.
16. Cash drawer should be locked in vault by cashier and supervisor.
17. Overs and shorts should be tracked.
18. ATM customers should be validated with card and PIN.
19. Cards should be seized if customer PIN wrong 3 times or if hot card is inserted.
20. ATM should be serviced under dual custody.
21. ATM should be filled by security personnel, under dual custody.
22. Removed cartridges should be secured and cash should be reconciled.
23. All electronic customers should be authenticated.
24. Unusual electronic transactions should be held until they can be verified.
25. Electronic customers should receive confirmation.

ANTICIPATED CONTROLS FOR ACCOUNT MAINTENANCE		
Completed by:	**Date:**	**Page of**

1. All customers should be authenticated.
2. All changes should be verified with customer.
3. All changes should be edited to ensure critical data is correct.
4. All critical changes should be confirmed by customer.
5. Old addresses with address correction requested should be used.
6. Accounts should be monitored after change for unusual activity or transactions.
7. Activity against inactive accounts should be investigated.
8. Change and close account procedures should be subjected to strong management review.
9. Closed accounts should be monitored by sales office and region to identify competitive position and customer service issues.
10. Errors should be subjected to second-party review.
11. Batches should be used to assist in balancing and reconciliation for manual transactions.
12. Transmittal documents should be used to ensure all batches sent out are received.
13. Electronic transactions should be authenticated and edited.
14. All inputs should be reconciled after consolidation.
15. Reconciliation should be performed of all updates, errors, etc.
16. Fraud sniffers should be used to detect potentially fraudulent activity.

ANTICIPATED CONTROLS FOR CASH AND CREDIT CARD SALES

Completed by:	Date:	Page of

1. Cashiers should count cash and negotiable instruments at beginning of shift.
2. Supervisor should verify count.
3. Cashier should use account name and password to log into system.
4. Supervisor should validate cashier.
5. Customer should be greeted and sale processed.
6. Cash should be counted and verified.
7. Debit card customers should be validated with card and PIN.
8. Cards should be seized if customer PIN wrong 3 times or if hot card is used.
9. All credit card transactions should be authorized by issuer.
10. Checks should be reviewed for completeness and accuracy before negotiation.
11. Cashier floor limits should be used for checks.
12. Supervisors should approve all transactions over the floor limit.
13. Cash should be picked up from cashier on a regular basis or when cash on hand exceeds prespecified limit.
14. Cash pick-up and drop-off should be recorded in system and on a separate log.
15. Cashier and supervisor should enter PIN or initial form to authenticate transaction.
16. Cashier should balance at end of shift.
17. Supervisor should review balancing.
18. Out-of-balance conditions should be reconciled.
19. Overs and shorts should be tracked.
20. If cashier fraud is suspected, security should be notified.

ANTICIPATED CONTROLS FOR SALES ORDER PROCESSING

Completed by:	Date:	Page of

1. All customer accounts should be verified.
2. Customer name and address should be verified.
3. Ship-to address should be verified.
4. Orders should not be taken for customers where the account is marked "NO NEW ORDERS UNTIL INVOICE IS PAID."
5. All manual orders should be keyed and edited to ensure critical data is correct.
6. All electronic and B2B transactions should be edited and errors sent back to the customer.
7. All telephone orders should be edited and errors corrected while the customer is on the line.
8. Customers should be advised of any out-of-stock items which would delay shipment.
9. All orders should have an order reference number.
10. All B2B transactions should be picked up from the service provider and edited to ensure no unauthorized transactions, files, or viruses are received.
11. B2B orders with errors should be sent back to the customer with an error reason code.
12. All web and shop-by-modem customers should be validated and authenticated.
13. Inventory should be checked before producing an order for a specific item.
14. If item is out of stock at one location, a search should be made to find the item in another warehouse.
15. Orders should be shipped from the closest warehouse to the customer.
16. Orders should be given a sequential order number, by shipping location.
17. Shipping location should check to ensure all orders are have been received.
18. Shortages should be recorded and sent to the invoicing area to ensure invoice is adjusted.

ANTICIPATED CONTROLS FOR SALES ORDER PROCESSING		
Completed by:	**Date:**	**Page** **of**

19. B2B customers should be sent a B2B shipping notice.
20. Orders should be removed from the open order file when they are shipped.
21. Invoices should be created for all on-account orders.
22. Pricing file should be checked periodically to ensure all prices are correct.
23. A reconciliation should be performed to ensure all orders were paid in advance or were invoiced.
24. Sales commission rates should be reviewed periodically.
25. State taxes should be collected for all required states and counties.
26. G/L posting should be performed daily.

ANTICIPATED CONTROLS FOR ADJUSTMENTS, CREDIT PROCESSING, AND RETURNS		
Completed by:	**Date:**	**Page** **of**

1. All credits and adjustments should be reviewed before processing.
2. Reasons for the credit or adjustment should be investigated.
3. Quality problems should be identified and fixed.
4. Credits and adjustments should be monitored and tracked by SR, customer, and shipping location.
5. Profitability impact of credits and adjustments should be monitored.
6. For returns, the reason should be clearly established.
7. Product should be inspected to determine if it can be resold.
8. Returns should only be accepted if proof of purchase accompanies the return.
9. Returns should be refunded based on the method of original payment (credit card refunded by credit card, etc.)

ANTICIPATED CONTROLS FOR PROMOTIONS		
Completed by:	**Date:**	**Page of**

1. All promotions and special pricing arrangements should be approved by the marketing group.
2. All promotional merchandise should be identified, so that it can not be returned for more money than it was purchased for.
3. Special discounts and allowances should conform to legislation.
4. Cooperative advertising programs should be monitored.
5. Customers must have proof of purchase to receive a rebate.
6. Rebates should not be made unless customer had sufficient volume to justify amount of rebate.

ANTICIPATED CONTROLS FOR CUSTOMER SERVICE		
Completed by:	**Date:**	**Page of**

1. Customer service surveys should be sent out periodically.
2. A professional survey firm should be used to design the survey and compile the results.

C. Risk Analysis

RISK ANALYSIS FOR SALES AND INVOICING		
Completed by:	**Date:**	**Page** **of**

1. Network penetration
2. Repudiated sales
3. Disclosure of customer data
4. Unauthorized update to web page (links to competitor)
5. Denial of service attacks
6. Inadequate new customer procedures
7. Poor credit approval
8. Poor separation of duties
9. Collusion
10. High returns
11. Bad checks
12. Disputed invoices
13. Excessive or unearned discounts
14. Poor customer maintenance
15. Automatic credit increases
16. Duplicate credit notes
17. Release of confidential information
18. Unrecorded sales
19. Fictitious sales
20. Delayed invoicing
21. Duplicate order processing
22. Duplicate shipping
23. Incomplete processing
24. Lost transactions
25. Poor customer service
26. Cash shortages
27. Lost orders
28. Excessive credit notes, adjustments, and returns
29. Short shipments
30. Damaged shipments
31. Selling to customers who cannot pay
32. Failure to automate
33. Labor intensiveness

D. Potential for Fraud

POTENTIAL FOR FRAUD		
Completed by:	**Date:**	**Page** **of**

1. Fictitious sales
2. Falsified ship-to address
3. Off-book sales
4. Off-register sales
5. False returns
6. False credit notes or adjustments
7. Diverted commissions
8. Substitution of credit notes for cash
9. Substitution of bad checks for cash
10. Credit and debit card fraud
11. Diverted shipments
12. Employee fraud
13. Customer fraud

E. Checklists

Checklist for New Accounts

No.	Question	Yes	No	WP XREF	REP XREF
1.	**Are there strong procedures over authorizing new customers?** **Do the procedures include:**				
	a. Completion of an application form?				
	b. Verification of customer credentials?				
	c. Database check to see if customer has previous unpaid bills?				
	d. Credit check for account sales?				
	e. Credit manager review and approval?				
	f. Credit manager sets initial credit limit?				
	g. Deposit for those with poor credit history?				
2.	**Does new customer information include the following:**				
	a. Name?				
	b. Address?				
	c. City, state, zip?				
	d. Home phone?				
	e. Business phone?				
	f. Social Security number?				
	g. Employment information?				
	h. Spouse's name and critical information?				
	i. Information concerning nearest relative or next of kin?				

(continues)

Checklist for New Accounts (Continued)

No.	Question	Yes	No	WP XREF	REP XREF
3.	**For new electronic B2B accounts, is there a trading partner agreement?** **Does it specify:**				
	a. Terms of the agreement?				
	b. Types of transactions?				
	c. Transmission windows?				
	d. Responsibilities of each party?				
4.	**Is there a test period for new B2B accounts?**				
	a. Is the data monitored for accuracy?				
	b. Are problems investigated and resolved promptly?				
Electronic Accounts					
5.	**Is the customer required to complete a registration form when first logging in to the web or a front-end application?**				
6.	**When a new account is requested, does the client complete an online application?**				
	a. Does the application contain all the required information?				
7.	**Is the information verified though company records or a credit report?**				
8.	**Is the completed application mailed to the client for signature**				
9.	**Is the client welcomed as a new customer?**				
	a. Online?				
	b. By mail?				

No.	Question	Yes	No	WP XREF	REP XREF
10.	Is the client given the option of paper or electronic statements?				
11.	Is the customer assigned a sales representative?				
12.	Is the customer's account monitored for an initial period?				
	New Account Process, Back Room				
13.	Is customer information verified if not already completed?				
14.	Is a search performed to see if the customer has other accounts with the company?				
	a. Are the accounts linked in the customer file?				
15.	Is a search conducted to see if the client has any old unpaid balances?				
16.	Is the confirmation prepared and sent to the client?				
17.	Is a new customer package prepared and sent to the client?				
18.	Is a customer service letter sent to the client two or three weeks after the account is opened?				

Checklist for Account Maintenance

No.	Question	Yes	No	WP XREF	REP XREF
1.	**Is the customer able to request changes:**				
	a. Over the phone?				
	b. In person?				
	c. By mail?				
	d. Electronically?				
2.	**Is the customer authenticated?**				
3.	**Is a copy of the change mailed to the customer?**				
	a. To the new address?				
	b. To the old address (Do not forward, address correction requested)?				
4.	**Are changes to ship-to and bill-to addresses verified with a known contact?**				
5.	**Are changes to inactive accounts closely monitored?**				
6.	**If customer is closing the account:**				
	a. Is the reason established?				
	b. Are attempts made to remedy any problems before closing?				
	c. Are arrangements made to pay any outstanding balances?				
7.	**If the company is closing the account:**				
	a. Is the customer notified why the account is being closed?				
	b. Is the account flagged to ensure it cannot be reopened without management approval?				

Checklist for Cash and Credit Card Sales

No.	Question	Yes	No	WP XREF	REP XREF
Cashier Start-Up Routine					
1.	**Are cashier's cash drawers secured when not in use?**				
	a. Is there a two-key procedure in place to remove cash drawer from storage?				
2.	**Are amounts counted when the drawer is removed from secure custody?**				
	a. Is the count performed by the cashier and a supervisor?				
3.	**Is a standard float used for cashier cash drawers?**				
	a. Are there controls over replenishment of standard float?				
4.	**Does the cashier log in using a password?**				
	a. Is a secondary password used?				
5.	**Does a supervisor enter an authorization code to log the cashier onto the cashier station?**				
6.	**Is the cashier float entered and verified by the cashier and supervisor?**				
Cashier-Based Customer Processing					
7.	**Is point-of-sale used for processing customer orders?**				
8.	**Does the cashier verify checks before accepting them?**				
	a. Numbers and figures agree and the check is not stale dated?				
	b. Account is not in hot check file?				
	c. Customer picture ID is reviewed and address is compared to address on check?				

(continues)

Checklist for Cash and Credit Card Sales (Continued)

No.	Question	Yes	No	WP XREF	REP XREF
9.	**Does a supervisor review checks over a certain limit or those that are suspicious?**				
10.	**If payment is by ATM card, does the customer enter PIN?**				
	a. Does the system connect to the bank to authenticate card and seek approval?				
	b. If the card is declined by the bank, is another form of payment requested, such as cash or credit card?				
	c. If the ATM card is rejected, is a customer's offer to pay by check declined?				
11.	**For credit card sales, does the system call the merchant bank for approval?**				
	a. If the transaction is declined, is another form of payment requested?				
	b. If the card is hot, does a secret call go out to the police?				
	Cash Pick-Up/Drop-Off				
12.	**Is a computer generated pick-up initiated when cash exceeds prespecified amounts?**				
13.	**Is there a manual procedure to pick up cash at regular intervals?**				
14.	**Is a computer transaction generated to record the cash pick-up or drop-off?**				
	a. Do both the cashier and supervisor enter their PINs to authenticate themselves and complete the transaction?				
15.	**Is a manual log of cash pick-up and drop-off maintained?**				
	a. Is it initialed by the cashier and the supervisor every time a transaction is recorded?				

No.	Question	Yes	No	WP XREF	REP XREF
	Cashier End of Shift				
16.	**Is a shift summary printed to aid in reconciliation?**				
17.	**Does the cashier perform the reconciliation?**				
18.	**Are out-of-balance situations reviewed and resolved?**				
19.	**Does the supervisor review or re-perform the reconciliation?**				
20.	**Is cash removed from the drawer or replaced with a standard float?**				
21.	**Is the drawer locked in the safe under dual custody?**				
22.	**Is an over and short report produced for each cashier?**				
	a. Is it reviewed by the supervisor?				
	b. Are significant items reviewed with the cashier?				
	c. Are overs and shorts tracked by cashier and supervisor to identify irregularities?				
	d. If fraud is suspected, is security notified?				
23.	**Is fraud software used to monitor unusual situations?**				
24.	**Is the over and short report reviewed by the supervisor?**				
	a. If fraud is suspected, is security notified?				
25.	**Is the head cashier's daily sales/cash report prepared?**				
	a. Is it reviewed by the manager?				
	b. Is software used to detect cash thefts by the head cashier?				

Checklist for Sales Order Processing

No.	Question	Yes	No	WP XREF	REP XREF
	Manual Transactions				
1.	**Can sales orders be taken using different mechanisms?**				
	a. By mail?				
	b. By fax?				
	c. By Sales Rep?				
	d. By telephone?				
	e. Using B2B?				
	f. Using a web page?				
	g. Using order-by-modem?				
2.	**Are all orders edited to ensure critical customer information is correct?**				
	a. Customer name and number?				
	b. Phone?				
	c. Bill-to address?				
	d. Product codes?				
	e. Ship-to address?				
	f. Delivery date?				
3.	**Are quantities ordered checked to the inventory database to ensure stock is available?**				
4.	**Are errors flagged and followed up immediately?**				
5.	**If goods are out of stock, is the customer notified?**				

No.	Question	Yes	No	WP XREF	REP XREF
	a. Is the customer given the option of back-ordering?				
6.	Are telephone orders recorded to provide verification and to resolve future problems?				
	B2B Transactions				
7.	Are there standard calling windows established?				
	a. Is the service provider called according to the window?				
8.	Are all transactions uploaded to a file?				
9.	Are the transactions sorted by record type and fed to the correct application?				
10.	Are the transactions edited?				
	a. Are errors reviewed to ensure they are not system errors?				
	b. Are any remaining errors sent back to the customer for resolution?				
11.	Are transactions converted to internal record format, then passed to the order process?				
	Web and Order-by-Modem Transactions				
12.	Is the customer validated and authenticated when logging in?				
13.	Can the customer view an electronic catalog?				
14.	Is the customer able to enter orders?				
	a. Is the customer requested to correct errors?				
	b. Is the order replayed after editing?				
	c. Is the data validated in real time?				

(continues)

Checklist for Sales Order Processing (Continued)

No.	Question	Yes	No	WP XREF	REP XREF
	d. Is the customer required to confirm the accuracy of the order?				
15.	**Is billing information entered by the customer?**				
	a. If a debit or credit card is used, is the card verified online by the merchant bank?				
	b. If payment is to be on account, is the account status and credit limit checked?				
	c. If paying by check, is the customer's past payment history reviewed?				
	Batch Order Processing				
16.	**If batch order processing is used, are all edited orders entered into a pending order file?**				
	a. Are batches read from the pending order file at the start of processing?				
17.	**Are all orders re-edited to ensure data integrity?**				
	a. Are errors rejected and placed in an error file?				
	b. Are errors reviewed on a timely basis?				
	c. Are corrections entered promptly?				
18.	**For each order, is the following checked:**				
	a. The order destination?				
	b. The nearest shipping point for that destination?				
	c. That enough stock is on hand at the shipping location for the order?				

No.	Question	Yes	No	WP XREF	REP XREF
19.	Are orders prepared and routed to the shipping location for printing and selection?				
20.	When goods are shipped, is the invoicing department sent a shipping confirmation?				
	a. Are any shipping discrepancies noted to enable adjustment of the customer's invoice?				
21.	Once the goods are shipped, is the order removed from the open order file to ensure it is not shipped twice?				
22.	If the item is not in stock at one location, is inventory checked at other locations?				
	a. Is the open purchases file checked to see when the additional quantities will be received?				
	Immediate Online Order Entry				
23.	Is online real-time ordering in use?				
24.	Are manual items entered and edited?				
	a. Are they released for immediate processing once they are correct?				
25.	Are web and shop-by-modem orders sent to an isolated server?				
	a. Is there a firewall between the web server and the host?				
	b. Has the firewall been audited using techniques developed by Canaudit?				
	c. Are transactions passed through the firewall to a filter?				
	d. Does the filter ensure that only transactions meeting the required filters are passed to the order processor?				

(continues)

Checklist for Sales Order Processing (Continued)

No.	Question	Yes	No	WP XREF	REP XREF
26.	**Is the B2B mailbox swept frequently for orders?**				
	a. Are they used to balance processing activity (polled less frequently when the system is busy, more frequently when the system is not)?				
27.	**Are all orders edited to ensure critical customer information is correct?**				
	a. Delivery date?				
	b. Customer name and number?				
	c. Phone?				
	d. Bill-to address?				
	e. Product codes?				
	f. Ship-to address?				
28.	**For each order, is the following information checked:**				
	a. The order destination?				
	b. The closest shipping point to the destination?				
29.	**If items are in stock:**				
	a. Is the inventory required to fill the order committed to the order?				
	b. Is the quantity on hand reduced by the amount committed?				
30.	**If items are not in stock, is the inventory at other locations checked?**				
	a. Is the item shipped from the alternate location if it is in stock?				

No.	Question	Yes	No	WP XREF	REP XREF
	b. Are open purchase orders checked?				
	c. Is the item back-ordered if it cannot be shipped from another location?				
31.	**Are orders routed to the warehouse or shipping location when the order is processed?**				
32.	**Are shortages recorded and sent to invoicing to adjust the invoice or for credit?**				
33.	**Is a shipping notice sent when the goods are shipped?**				
	a. Mail?				
	c. E-mail?				
	d. B2B?				

Checklist for Invoicing

No.	Question	Yes	No	WP XREF	REP XREF
1.	**Is invoicing performed at the time the order is received?**				
	a. Is the invoice sent out immediately?				
2.	**If not:**				
	a. Is the invoice sent to arrive a day before the goods do?				
	b. If not, does management realize they are not maximizing cash flow?				
3.	**Is the order invoiced using the prices that will be in effect when the order is shipped?**				
	a. For price advances?				
	b. For price declines?				
4.	**Is the order invoiced using the customer's designated price category?**				
5.	**If orders are adjusted by the customer before invoicing, is the adjustment reflected on the invoice?**				
6.	**Is there a reconciliation between items ordered, items shipped, and items invoiced?**				
	a. Is it automated?				
7.	**Are sales commissions calculated at the time the order is invoiced?**				
	a. Can commissions be diverted from CSRs (not commissioned) to SRs (commissioned)?				
8.	**Is sales tax added to the invoice?**				
	a. Using the correct rate for the customer's state?				

No.	Question	Yes	No	WP XREF	REP XREF
9.	Are sales taxes computed by state, balanced, and transferred to payables?				
	a. Could the taxes be diverted to another vendor or employee?				
10.	Is the general ledger updated with the sales, taxes payable, commissions, etc.?				

Checklist for Adjustments, Credits, and Returns

No.	Question	Yes	No	WP XREF	REP XREF
1.	**Are adjustments gathered by type and source?**				
	a. Shipping adjustments?				
	b. Pricing adjustments?				
2.	**Are adjustments reviewed and approved before they are processed?**				
3.	**Are approved adjustments transferred to invoicing for processing?**				
4.	**Are there controls to ensure the adjustment is processed to the correct account?**				
5.	**Are credit notes created for valid reasons?**				
	a. Damaged goods?				
	c. Pricing errors?				
	d. Shortages upon receipt?				
6.	**Are credit notes approved by the sales manager?**				
	a. Are credit notes for short-shipped and damaged goods also approved by the warehouse manager?				
7.	**Are credit notes ever rejected?**				
8.	**Are items returned for valid reasons?**				
9.	**Is the returned product inspected for damage?**				
10.	**Is a check made to ensure a credit or adjustment was not already made for the returned item?**				

No.	Question	Yes	No	WP XREF	REP XREF
11.	If the returned item is to be refunded, is the refund made in the same form as the purchase (i.e., credit card adjustment for credit card payment)?				
12.	Does management receive regular reports on adjustments, credits, and returned items?				
	a. Are efforts made to identify clients or SRs who abuse these transactions?				
	b. Is a trend analysis performed to monitor the volume of these transactions relative to sales?				

Checklist for Promotions

No.	Question	Yes	No	WP XREF	REP XREF
1.	**Are promotion programs created by the marketing group?**				
	a. Is the sales volume estimated?				
	b. Is a profitability analysis performed?				
	c. Is a new UPC code created and registered to prevent twofers being returned as onefers?				
2.	**For special discounts and allowances:**				
	a. Are terms and conditions agreed?				
	b. Is the pricing table updated with the new discounts and allowances?				
3.	**For cooperative advertising, are ads sent in with the invoice?**				
	a. Is the Audit Bureau of Publications checked to determine circulation?				
	b. If approved, are the cooperative advertising funds entered into the invoicing system to give the client credit?				
4.	**For rebates, are checks made to ensure sufficient stock was purchased to justify the rebate?**				
5.	**Are the effectiveness of the above programs tracked and analyzed?**				
	a. Are the programs still required?				
	b. Can the amounts be reduced without affecting profitability?				

Checklist for Customer Service

No.	Question	Yes	No	WP XREF	REP XREF
1.	Is customer service a key organizational goal?				
	a. Is management committed to improving customer service and responsiveness?				
2.	Are customer surveys sent out for:				
	a. New accounts?				
	b. Closed accounts?				
	c. Random sample basis?				
3.	Are surveys sent to an outside service for compilation and processing?				
4.	Are customer service reports produced for management and reviewed?				
5.	Is service quality monitored to identify improvements or service deterioration?				
	a. Does management take action when service quality is degrading?				
	b. Does management congratulate staff when service quality improves?				

F. Risk/Control Tables

Risk/Control Table for New Customer Accounts

Risk	Control	Status
New customer information may be entered incorrectly or the customer may provide incorrect data. This could result in poor customer service or fraud.	Use strong edit routines to ensure that all required information is entered. Also, edit the data to ensure that it is accurate. Ask for identification and verify critical data. Perform a zip code and address match to ensure the correct zip is entered for the address. Look up the customer in the Customer database to determine if the customer is preexisting and verify critical information. Check to see if customer had a closed account and determine reason for closing. Use a product such as PHONE DISC POWER FINDER to ensure that the phone number, name, and address are correct. You could also use an automated Internet white pages hookup to confirm the phone number and address. Send a confirmation to the customer to verify the information is correct. Run a credit report to verify critical information for larger accounts.	

Risk	Control	Status
Required documentation may not be completed and signed.	Ensure all account documentation is completed and signed. Have a second party review the new account application.	
For B2B accounts, the trading partner agreement replaces the terms and conditions that appeared on paper purchase orders. A failure to have a trading partner agreement may result in uncollectible receivables and civil litigation.	A trading partner agreement should be signed with all B2B customers. It should include: 1. The terms of the agreement 2. The types of transactions covered by the agreement 3. The transmission windows 4. The responsibilities of each party 5. The need for security and confidentiality	
The customer may experience delivery interruptions if new B2B accounts do not have an initial test period.	There should be an initial test period for new B2B accounts. Orders should be processed in parallel until the test is completed. The test data should be closely monitored for errors and any problems should be investigated and resolved.	
New web and order-by-modem customers may not have a legal contract, making debts uncollectible and resulting in civil litigation.	There should be a registration form for first time electronic users. The form should contain all the required new customer information. The customer should select the method of payment as part of the registration process. If the payment is C.O.D. or on account, a credit check should be run.	

(continues)

Risk/Control Table for New Customer Accounts (Continued)

Risk	Control	Status
	A copy of the registration form and a new customer agreement should be mailed to the customer for signature. The first order may be processed before the form is returned.	
Credit and debit card information could be monitored as it crosses the Internet. This could result in a fraud.	Until a standard emerges for encrypting credit and debit cards across the Internet, the company should provide the electronic customer with an ordering software kit, which has embedded encryption for the credit and debit card.	
	No claims should be made about encrypted information as the encryption code could be beaten.	
A failure to confirm client information may result in a fraud or the inability to collect for goods shipped.	A back room process should ensure all new customers are verified, that they do not have old unpaid balances, and that the information provided on the credit application is correct.	
	A letter should be sent to the new customer confirming the information and welcoming them as a new customer.	

Risk/Control Table for Account Maintenance

Risk	Control	Status
A fraud could result from unauthorized changes to customer account information.	Customers should be verified before changes are accepted. Changes should only be made by approved personnel. For address changes, the confirmation should be sent to the old address with DO NOT FORWARD and ADDRESS CORRECTION REQUESTED on the envelope. This will cause the post office to forward the address change to the company for verification. The confirmation could also be sent to the new address, however this would only verify valid changes by the customer, not fraudulent changes by others. Accounts should be monitored for a period of time after the change has been made to determine if there are any unusual changes.	
Errors could be made during the change process that might go undetected.	Changes should be subjected to strong edit routines. Errors should be flashed on screen immediately, so they can be corrected. There should be management approval for changes to large volume accounts or VIP accounts.	

Risk/Control Table for Cash and Credit Card Sales

Risk	Control	Status
Without strong cash control procedures, the company is exposed to loss, theft, and wrongful termination suits.	All cash drawers should be secured when not in use. Cash should be counted under dual custody at the start of a cashier's shift or when the cash drawer is removed from safekeeping. The cashier's float should be entered into the system as part of the login process. The cashier should be required to log in to the system with a user ID and password. In areas with a large cash exposure, a supervisor should be required to authorize a cashier login by entering the supervisor's password or PIN. Procedures should be in place to remove excess cash periodically from the cashier's drawer. When cash is removed, the amount should be entered into the system and the cashier and the supervisor should be required to enter their passwords or PINs to validate the transaction. In addition, a manual log slip should be completed in case of a system failure or disagreement. The same procedures should be in place to provide additional cash to cashiers. Cameras should be used to monitor employees and to identify thieves.	

Risk	Control	Status
	At the end of the shift, the cashier's cash and checks should be counted and reconciled. Once the cashier has completed the count, a supervisor should verify the count and investigate any balancing discrepancies.	
	The cash should be removed from the drawer at the end of the shift. Some companies like to place the standard float in the drawer so it is ready for the next day. If this is done, the drawer should be locked in the safe.	
	An over and short report should be used to monitor cash overages and shortages. Security may need to be called in if there are patterns that indicate theft of cash.	
Dishonored checks are a direct hit to the bottom line. Not only is the amount of the check not recovered, but collection costs can be as much as 50 percent of the value of the check.	The cashier should verify that the check is properly completed: 1. The numbers and figures should agree. 2. It should not be stale dated. 3. It should not be altered. 4. It should be payable to the company. 5. It should be signed by the payer. 6. The address on the check should agree with the address on the customer's picture ID. 7. It should not be in the hot card list.	

(continues)

Risk/Control Table for Cash and Credit Card Sales (Continued)

Risk	Control	Status
	8. The customer's picture ID should be checked. The supervisor should be called to approve any checks over a certain amount, any checks not meeting the above conditions, or company checks being cashed by a customer who is not a regular customer. Bad checks should be monitored by cashier and location. They can be used to cover a cash theft if the cashier or supervisor brings in a bad check and uses it to replace cash taken from the cash drawer.	
A failure to authorize credit and debit card transactions through the merchant bank may result in the payment being rejected.	The system should automatically call the merchant bank for approval of credit and debit card transactions. For debit cards, the customer will have to enter their PIN. If the card is approved, the sale should proceed. If the card is not approved, the customer should be asked for another form of payment. If an ATM card is declined, the cashier should not accept a check without the supervisor's approval. If the card is a hot card, the supervisor should be called to assist or a silent alarm should bring security personnel.	

Risk	Control	Status
The daily sales and cash report may not be completed correctly. This could be the result of a head cashier or supervisor fraud or errors in completing the form.	The daily cash report should be reviewed to ensure that the person completing it is not using rolling deposits to cover a cash theft. (A rolling deposit allows a person to take funds after the last bank deposit of the day, and cover it up with cash received the next morning).	
	A surprise daily sales report/ cash count and reconciliation should be performed by regional security on a rotating basis.	
A failure to make timely deposits may result in poor float management and increase the loss in the event of a robbery.	Deposits should be made at least once a day and more frequently if merited. An armored service should be used if large amounts of cash are involved.	
	If deposits are taken to the bank by staff (or cash and coin are picked up) and large amounts are involved, dual custody procedures should be used.	

Risk/Control Table for Sales Order Processing

Risk	Control	Status
A failure to automate the ordering process increases the cost of doing business and may also result in loss of competitive advantage.	The use of B2B should be required for all large clients. We are now past the experimentation phase and most companies now have this capability. For smaller clients, electronic ordering, order-by-modem, and web site orders should be used wherever possible. • The automation of manual orders can be handled in several ways, These are: • The use of a B2B service provider to key orders into B2B transaction format. • Providing the customer with an 800 number for faxing orders to a central site. The selected site can be in an area where employment costs are low and there is a well-educated work force (central California, North Dakota, Bombay, Winnipeg, etc.). The orders may be imaged if a standard form is used or keyed and verified. The secret is to automate the process at the earliest possible point. • Use a centralized phone center to take phone orders. Again, select a site that has low costs and high skills. For large organizations, two call centers should be used in case phone lines are severed to one location and to take advantage of time zones.	

Risk	Control	Status
B2B transactions may not be sent to the service provider on time; orders may not be picked up from the provider on time; and there could be errors in the conversion process.	The customer and the company should adhere to transmission windows to ensure that orders are received promptly. The orders should be converted from the B2B format into order system format and edited to ensure the conversion was accurate. To reduce the likelihood of system penetration and viruses, a filter should be used to filter all transactions from the B2B service provider. Any records that do not conform to the B2B standard should be dropped.	
The system is exposed to hackers if web sites and order-by-modem techniques are used.	Isolate these services onto separate servers. Ensure all users are authenticated and that the security on the machine prevents them from navigating the information superhighway. (See Section 2 of the Audit Guide.) Use filters to edit inbound data to ensure files are not being transferred. Use a tested firewall that has been audited using the techniques in the Canaudit seminar, "Control and Security of Telecommunications Networks" and my book *Network Security: A Control Assessment Approach* to ensure communications between the server and the host are protected.	

(continues)

Risk/Control Table for Sales Order Processing (Continued)

Risk	Control	Status
	Use filters on the host to ensure that all transactions from the server conform to preestablished data formats.	
	Be ever vigilant for hackers attempting to penetrate the server.	
If orders are not edited, errors will occur that can delay the order, increase returns, and degrade customer service.	All orders should be validated and critical information should be edited. Items that fail the edit checks should be rejected.	
	Errors should be investigated and corrected as soon as possible. For telephone and web site transactions, the best time to detect an error is while the customer is still online. This enables the customer to provide corrected information.	
If orders are not shipped from the closest location to the customer, shipping costs will be higher, resulting in less profit from the transaction.	Orders should be shipped from the closest location to the client, if possible. If the item is out of stock, it should be shipped from another location.	
Stocking slow-moving items in every location greatly increases the inventory costs and the risk of obsolescence.	Whenever possible, stock slow movers in a central location. Use UPS or Federal Express to ship these products to the customer. Federal Express Logistical Services also can be used to warehouse and ship slow moving items.	

Risk	Control	Status
If orders are printed and then delivered to the shipping location, there is a risk that the orders could be lost. In addition, the delivery process increases the total time to process and ship the order.	Orders should be transmitted to the shipping location.	
If short shipments occur and the invoice is not adjusted, the customer may delay payment.	If a product is short shipped, the invoicing department should be notified to adjust the billing.	

Risk/Control Table for Invoicing, Adjustments, and Credits

Risk	Control	Status
If invoicing is not performed at the right point in time, there are several risks. First, if the invoice is too late, there will be a negative impact on cash flow. If it is produced too early, short shipments and price changes may necessitate invoice adjustments.	Invoices should be created as soon as reliable inventory and pricing information is available for the goods ordered. If orders are turned around in one or two days, invoices should be created when the order is prepared for selection.	
	The invoice should be timed to arrive at the client's office at about the same time as the goods. If goods will take two or three days to arrive at the customer's location, the invoice should be mailed to arrive when the goods do.	
	For B2B shipments, the invoice should be sent to the customer (via the B2B service provider) when the goods are shipped.	
Order adjustments due to short shipping the customer could cause the customer to run out of stock. This jeopardizes customer service and may result in lost customers.	Out-of-stock conditions should be detected at the order processing stage. However, if they are not, the customer should be notified (by B2B, fax, web) of the adjustment. The invoice should also be updated to reflect the adjustment. To speed this process, the company may consider permitting invoicing adjustments from the shipping location via an online or client/server process.	
	The customer should also be able to adjust an order up to	

Risk	Control	Status
	the point of selection and invoicing. This option could be available to B2B customers.	
Pricing errors can also delay payment of the invoice and result in poor customer service.	The order should be invoiced using the customer's designated pricing category and the prices in effect at the time the order was/will be shipped.	
If orders, shipments, and invoicing are not reconciled, there is a risk of unbilled shipments, shipments invoiced but not shipped, and orders invoiced twice.	An automated reconciliation should be performed at least daily to ensure that invoicing is correct. There should be an investigation into any unreconciled items.	
Sales commissions may be incorrect due to returns, credits, adjustments, and diverted commissions.	Commissions should be calculated and transferred to the payroll system, either when the order is invoiced or on a daily or weekly basis. If there are any returns, adjustments, or credits, they should be deducted from the commission.	
	Controls should be established to prevent commissions being diverted (CSR sales are not commissionable, so the CSR enters the SR as the sales person and the SR gets commission.)	
Sales taxes may be required, but may not be invoiced. Also, taxes invoiced may not be remitted.	Sales taxes should be computed by state, balanced and reconciled. Controls should be implemented to ensure that the taxable amounts are remitted to the state and not diverted.	

(continues)

Risk/Control Table for Invoicing, Adjustments, and Credits (Continued)

Risk	Control	Status
Freight costs may be the responsibility of the client, yet they may not be invoiced.	If shipping costs are to be billed to the client, this should be recorded in the customer record. The program should automatically charge freight when the invoice is being created.	
A failure to control credits, adjustments, and returns could result in lost business as well as lost profits.	These items should be monitored and tracked by customer, salesperson, and product. A trend or regression analysis should be used to identify potential abuse.	
	Quality control should review the reasons for the credits and returns to identify quality problems and to develop solutions.	

Risk/Control Table for Promotions

Risk	Control	Status
Promotional programs are subject to abuse. Customers may take discounts and rebates they are not entitled to. They may return two-for-one items individually for full credit, receiving a rebate for more product than they purchased.	All promotional programs should be created by the marketing group. This will ensure that all programs are authorized and will be consistently offered to all clients. There should be a formal agreement between the customer and the client concerning special discounts and allowances. Each client program should be monitored to ensure that the account remains profitable after all credits, returns, discounts, allowances, rebates, cooperative advertising, and other incentives are included in the customer profitability analysis. The effectiveness of these programs should be tracked. Unless solid benefits can be proven, then consideration should be given to eliminating some or all of these programs in favor of lower pricing across the board.	
The company may be paying for cooperative advertising that never ran.	A copy of the ad should be sent in with the invoice for all cooperative advertising. Occasionally, a check should be made of local and regional newspapers to ensure the ad ran. Also, the newspaper can directly bill the company for its portion of the cooperative advertising.	

Risk/Control Table for Customer Service

Risk	Control	Status
A failure to monitor customer service could result in long-term business loss.	Customer service should be monitored on a regular basis using a professional survey firm.	

G. Cash Flow Potential

ITEMS WITH CASH FLOW POTENTIAL		
Completed by:	**Date:**	**Page of**

Real Example of Invoicing Delay

Initial delay from shipping to the invoicing procedure	1 day
Invoicing and mailing delay	1 day
Postal delay	3 days
Customer mail delay	1 day
A/P processing delay	<u>1 day</u>
Total technical delay	7 days
Actual delay	9 days
Delivery time frame	<u>2 days</u>
Net invoicing delay	7 days
Average daily sales	$ 4,477,180
Net invoicing delay	<u>× 7</u>
Cash flow potential (invoice 7 days before shipping)	**$31,340,260**

ITEMS WITH CASH FLOW POTENTIAL		
Completed by:	**Date:**	**Page of**

Real Example of B2B Labor Savings

Order Origination Process

Item	Resources	Cost
Mail pick-up	½ person @ 60,000	$ 30,000
Vehicle	⅙ of 48,000	8,000
Mail room activity	2 people @ 50,000	100,000
Data entry activity	3.5 people @ 40,000	140,000
Sales desk	4 people @ 40,000	160,000
Credit desk	2 people @ 60,000	120,000
Computer operations	1 person @ 70,000	70,000
Postage	500,000 @ 37 cents	185,000
Invoices and envelopes	500,000 @ 15 cents	75,000
Total sales order costs		$898,000

Cash Receipts Process

Item	Resources	Cost
Mail pick-up	½ person @ 60,000	$ 30,000
Vehicle	⅙ of 48,000	8,000
Mail room activity	2 people @ 60,000	120,000
Data entry activity	2 people @ 40,000	80,000
A/R activity	4 people @ 40,000	160,000
Collections	2 people @ 60,000	120,000
Computer operations	1 person @ 70,000	70,000
Bank reconciliation	1 person @ 40,000	40,000
Bank processing fees	500,000 @ 40 cents	200,000
Record retention costs	10,000 sq. ft. @ 25	250,000
Office space	12,000 sq. ft @ 25	300,000
Annual external audit fee		50,000
Annual internal audit charges		150,000
Total cash receipts costs		$1,578,000
Management staff	4 people @ 120,000	$ 480,000
Total cost of the entire process		**$2,946,000**
Total potential for errors (estimated)		32 places

Sales Order Process after Re-engineering

Item	Resources	Cost
Data entry activity	1 person @ 40,000	$ 40,000
Sales desk	1 person @ 40,000	40,000
Computer operations	¼ person @ 70,000 (approximate)	17,500
B2B mail box charges	375,000 @ 10 cents (approximate)	37,500
B2B services (manual)	125,000 @ 55 cents	68,750
Total sales order costs		$203,750

Cash Receipts Process

Item	Resources	Cost
A/R activity	2 people @ 40,000	$ 160,000
Collections	2 people @ 60,000	120,000
Computer operations	¼ person @ 70,000	17,500
Bank reconciliation	1 person @ 40,000	40,000
Bank processing fees	375,000 @ 10 cents	37,500
Lock box, manual items	125,000 @ 50 cents	62,500
Office space	3,000 sq. ft @ 25	75,000
Annual external audit fee		25,000
Annual internal audit charges		75,000
Total cash receipts costs		$ 612,000
Management staff	2 people @120,000	$ 240,000
Total cost of the entire process		**$1,082,750**
Cost of the old process		(2,946,000)
Savings		**$1,863,250**
Effect on earnings per share (1,863,250 ÷ 55,000,000)		3.3 cents
Effect on stock price (3.3 × 12)		39.6 cents

ITEMS WITH CASH FLOW POTENTIAL		
Completed by:	**Date:**	**Page of**

1. Invoicing sooner.
2. Moving to B2B for larger customers.
3. Implementing web order sites and order-by-phone to reduce labor for smaller customer orders.
4. Using 800 numbers for order-by-fax.
5. Placing manual order transcription and phone order centers in low-cost areas.
6. Installing fraud prevention programs.
7. Moving walk-in customers away from checks and into credit and debit cards.
8. Making deposits more frequently.
9. Moving from batch order processing to real time client/server processing.
10. Reducing returns by improving quality.
11. Reducing adjustments by improving shipping reliability and inventory control.
12. Storing slow moving items in one location for consolidated shipping.
13. Reducing the number of rebates and special promotion programs.

H. Audit Software Tests and Specifications

This section has two components: a list of suggested audit tests and the design specifications for the most common tests to get you started.

Select the tests you believe are necessary from the following list and then add any additional tests that your company requires.

Suggested Audit Tests	Design Specifications
Foot file	List shipments on hold
Profitability analysis	Calculate invoicing delay
Credit note analysis	Compare discounts to terms
Discount analysis	List discounts taken, not earned
Missing required data	List unusual discount terms
Trace sales invoice to receivable	Credit limit analysis
Trace receivable to sales invoice	Sum subsidiary ledger to control
Trace activity to GL	account

Objective: Identify Accounts with Missing Data

REQUIRED DATA ELEMENTS

Sales office   Customer name   Account
Social Security number   Address   Zip
Phone   Account balance

EXTRACT AND SORT CRITERIA

Select if any name, address, Social Security number, zip, or phone is blank.
Sort by sales office, customer name.

CALCULATIONS

Test to see if fields are blank, if so, place a 1 in missing data.

SAMPLE REPORT

List of Accounts with Missing Data

Sales Office	Account Number	Name	Address	Zip	Phone	Social Security Number	Account Balance
		John Doe	Address	Zip	Phone	SSN	
		X if blank	X if blank	X if blank	X if blank	X if blank	
		Count of missing	Count of missing	Count of missing	Count of missing	Count of missing	Total

Page Breaks and Spacing

1. Page break on Sales Office so that report can be distributed to each Sales Office.

Objective: Identify Customer Who May Be Perpetrating Bankruptcy Fraud

REQUIRED DATA ELEMENTS

Sales office	Account	Average shipments
Balance	Account status	Current shipments
Last payment	Customer name	

EXTRACT AND SORT CRITERIA

Select accounts with status = or > 60 days and current shipments
> (average shipments × 1.25)

Sort by customer

CALCULATIONS

Excess percentage = current shipments ÷ average shipments

SAMPLE REPORT AND DATABASE

List of Customers Who May Be Perpetrating Bankruptcy Fraud

Sales Office	Customer Name	Account Number	Average Shipments	Current Shipments	Excess Percentage	Account Balance	Last Payment Date
		Count				Total	

Page Breaks and Spacing

1. Page break on Sales Office.

NOTE: In addition to printing report, this information is to be written to a database called dormant.

Objective: Profitability Analysis by Sales Representative

REQUIRED DATA ELEMENTS		
Sales representative	Account	Total sales
Cost of goods sold	Discounts	Allowances
Rebates	Cooperative advertising	Returns
Commissions	Customer name	

EXTRACT AND SORT CRITERIA
All customers
Sort by sales representative and percentage profitability (low to high)

CALCULATIONS
Total discounts = discounts + allowances + rebates
Profitability (sales − cogs − total discounts − returns − commissions − coop advertising)
Profitability percentage = profitability ÷ total sales

SAMPLE REPORT

Profitability Analysis by Sales Representative

Sales Person	Profitability Percentage	Account Number	Total Sales	Cost of Goods Sold	Total Discounts	Returns	Commissions	Cooperative Advertising
			Total		Total			Total

Objective: Discount Analysis by Sales Representative

REQUIRED DATA ELEMENTS

Sales representative	Account	Total sales
Cost of goods sold	Discounts	Allowances
Rebates	Cooperative advertising	Returns
Commissions	Customer name	

EXTRACT AND SORT CRITERIA

All customers

Sort by sales representative and total discount percentage

CALCULATIONS

Total discounts = discounts + allowances + rebates

Discount percentage total discounts ÷ total sales

SAMPLE REPORT

Discount Analysis by Sales Representative

Sales Person	Discount Percentage	Account Number	Total Sales	Cost of Goods Sold	Total Discounts	Returns	Commissions	Cooperative Advertising
			Total		Total			Total

Objective: Credit Note Analysis by Sales Representative

REQUIRED DATA ELEMENTS

Sales representative	Account	Total sales
Cost of goods sold	Discounts	Allowances
Rebates	Cooperative advertising	Returns
Credit Notes	Customer name	

EXTRACT AND SORT CRITERIA

All customers

Sort by sales representative and credit note percentage

CALCULATIONS

Credit note percentage = credit notes ÷ total sales

Total discounts = discounts + allowances + rebates

SAMPLE REPORT

Credit Note Analysis by Sales Representative

Sales Person	Credit Note Percentage	Account Number	Total Sales	Credit Notes	Total Discounts	Returns	Commissions	Cooperative Advertising
		Total	Total	Total			Total	

Objective: Identify Customers Over Credit Limit
Who Have Orders to Be Shipped

REQUIRED DATA ELEMENTS

Sales representative	Account	Balance
Credit limit	Value of unshipped orders	Last payment date
Order pending flag	Customer name	

EXTRACT AND SORT CRITERIA

Select customers with balance > credit limit $\times$ 1.05 and order pending flag = 'Y'

Sort by branch, date of last transaction

CALCULATIONS

Excess = balance − credit limit

SAMPLE REPORT AND DATABASE

List of Customers Over Credit Limit Who Have Orders to Be Shipped

Sales Representative	Account	Balance	Credit Limit	Value of Unshipped Orders	Last Payment Date	Customer Name	----------
					Enter **X** if dormant code not present		
		Total	Total	Total			

Page Breaks and Spacing

1. Page break on Sales Rep so sales can be analyzed by representative.

Index